William Fraser Rae

**Newfoundland to Manitoba**

Through Canada's Maritime, Mining, and Prairie Provinces

William Fraser Rae

**Newfoundland to Manitoba**
*Through Canada's Maritime, Mining, and Prairie Provinces*

ISBN/EAN: 9783744759045

Printed in Europe, USA, Canada, Australia, Japan

Cover: Foto ©Andreas Hilbeck / pixelio.de

More available books at **www.hansebooks.com**

# NEWFOUNDLAND TO MANITOBA

THROUGH

CANADA'S MARITIME, MINING, AND PRAIRIE PROVINCES

BY

W. FRASER RAE

WITH MAPS AND ILLUSTRATIONS

NEW YORK
G. P. PUTNAM'S SONS
27 AND 29 WEST 23D STREET
1881

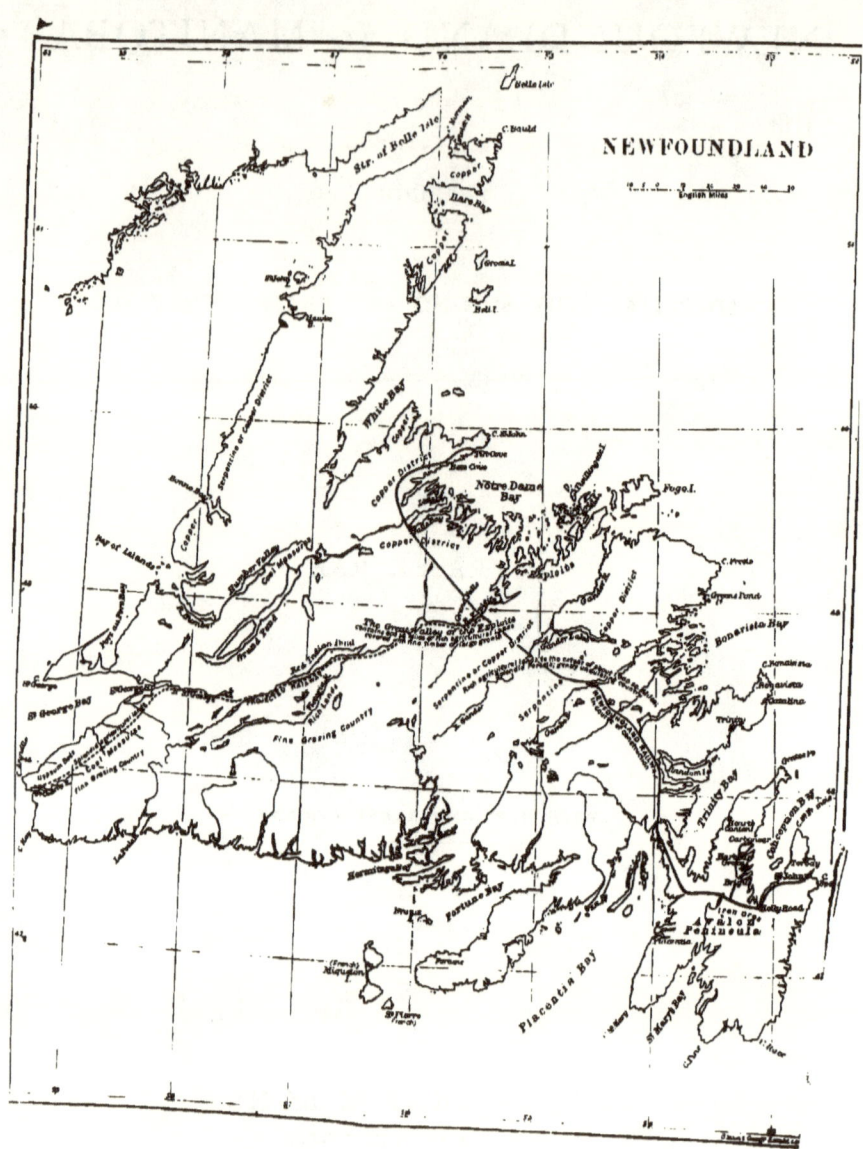

# PREFACE.

I VISITED and described the Province of Manitoba and a part of the New West in the United States, as a Correspondent of *The Times*, during the summer and autumn of 1878. Last autumn and winter I visited Newfoundland, landed on the North American continent, journeyed across it from Halifax on the Atlantic Ocean to Rapid City on the Little Saskatchewan River, and athwart it from the Red River of the North in Manitoba to the Rio Grande in New Mexico. Letters contributed to *The Times*, during both visits, are reprinted in the following pages. All of these letters have been carefully revised; some have been recast, while the contents of many pages now appear for the first time. The Province of British Columbia is the only important section of the Dominion which is not treated in this work.

I purpose reproducing in another volume my experiences and observations in those States and Territories of the Union which constitute the remarkable New West, extending from the Territory of Dakota to the Territory of New Mexico, and from the State of Kansas to the Territory of Wyoming.

Whilst gratefully acknowledging my indebtedness to many Canadians for great courtesy and attention, I must return special thanks for the information and aid which I received from Mr. John Lowe, Secretary to the Department of Agriculture at Ottawa, and Mr. William Hespeler, Dominion Immigration Agent at Winnipeg. Mr. Hespeler is one of the many cultured Germans who have made Canada their home, who do credit to the country of their birth, and who render genuine and patriotic service to the land of their adoption.

# CONTENTS.

## CHAPTER I.
### ENGLAND'S OLDEST COLONY.

|   | PAGE |
|---|---|
| Earliest Notices of Newfoundland | 3 |
| Products of the Island | 5 |
| Rich in Minerals | 7 |
| Sir Humphrey Gilbert's Mission | 9 |
| Daniel discovers Silver | 11 |
| Result of Mineral Discoveries | 13 |
| Whitbourne's Account | 15 |
| First Colonists | 17 |
| Laws of Charles I. | 19 |
| Settlement Impeded | 21 |
| Condition of the Fishermen | 23 |
| Increase of Pauperism | 25 |
| Responsible Government granted | 27 |
| Views of the Islanders | 29 |
| The Capital of Newfoundland | 31 |
| Public Buildings | 33 |
| Legislative Assembly | 35 |
| The Soil and Climate | 37 |
| Newfoundland Railway | 39 |
| Agricultural Prospects | 41 |
| Opposition to a Railway | 43 |
| Newspaper Press | 45 |
| Notes on Newspapers | 47 |
| Compulsory Education | 49 |
| Principal Imports | 51 |
| Mines and Mining | 53 |
| French Claims | 55 |
| Fish, Game, and Dogs | 57 |

## CHAPTER II.
### THE LAND OF THE "BLUE NOSES."

|   |   |
|---|---|
| The Founder of Nova Scotia | 61 |
| The "National Policy" | 63 |
| "Old Fossils" | 65 |
| Gold-Mines | 67 |

## Contents.

|  | PAGE |
|---|---|
| Nova Scotian Collieries | 69 |
| Scenery and Climate | 71 |
| The Capital of Nova Scotia | 73 |
| Halifax Hospitality | 75 |
| Governor Archibald | 77 |

### CHAPTER III.
#### THE PROVINCE OF NEW BRUNSWICK.

|  |  |
|---|---|
| The Puritans and New Brunswick | 81 |
| Foundation of St. John | 83 |
| New Denmark | 85 |
| The St. John River | 87 |
| Churches in Fredericton | 89 |
| Headquarters of the Intercolonial | 91 |
| A Forest on Fire | 93 |
| New Brunswick Land Laws | 95 |
| Cattle-Rearing | 97 |

### CHAPTER IV.
#### PRINCE EDWARD ISLAND.

|  |  |
|---|---|
| Oysters, Mackerel, and Lobsters | 101 |
| Yield and price of Potatoes | 103 |
| Highland Settlers | 105 |
| Subdivision of the Land | 107 |
| Landlords and Tenants | 109 |
| Settlement of the Land Question | 111 |
| Summerside | 113 |
| Charlottetown and its Suburbs | 115 |
| Governor John Ready's Administration | 117 |

### CHAPTER V.
#### INTERCOLONIAL, GRAND TRUNK, AND NORTHERN RAILWAYS.

|  |  |
|---|---|
| Intercolonial: Origin and Character | 121 |
| Workshops at Moncton | 123 |
| Scenery along the Line | 125 |
| Newcastle | 127 |
| Mr. Justice Henry | 129 |
| Mr. Hickson's Management of Grand Trunk | 131 |
| Glut of Traffic | 133 |
| Muskoka Lakes | 135 |
| Future Prospects of Northern Railway | 137 |

### CHAPTER VI.
#### ACROSS LAKE SUPERIOR.

|  |  |
|---|---|
| The North Shore Route | 139 |
| A Landlord's Career | 141 |

## Contents.

|  | PAGE |
|---|---|
| Tempestuous Weather | 143 |
| The Bruce Mines | 145 |
| Homes for Indian Children | 147 |
| Fishing in the Rapids | 149 |
| A Historic Ceremony | 151 |
| Panegyric on Louis XIV. | 153 |
| Michipicoten Island | 155 |
| Discoveries of Copper | 157 |
| Value of Native Copper | 159 |
| Copper Mining Companies | 161 |
| Mineral Riches | 163 |
| Silver, Copper, and Iron Deposits | 165 |

### CHAPTER VII.
#### DULUTH TO WINNIPEG.

| | |
|---|---|
| Mr. Proctor Knott's Speech | 169 |
| Delights of Duluth | 171 |
| Geographical Ignorance | 173 |
| Manufactures and Trade | 175 |
| Land Speculators | 177 |
| A Hint to Emigrants | 179 |

### CHAPTER VIII.
#### ON THE RED RIVER OF THE NORTH.

| | |
|---|---|
| Course of the Red River | 181 |
| Mammoth Farms | 183 |
| By Water to Winnipeg | 185 |
| Lake Minnetonka | 187 |
| Stern Wheel Steamers | 189 |
| Onslaughts of Insects | 191 |
| Scenery on the Banks | 193 |
| First View of Winnipeg | 195 |

### CHAPTER IX.
#### THE CITY OF WINNIPEG.

| | |
|---|---|
| University of Manitoba | 199 |
| Historical and Scientific Society | 201 |
| Public Markets | 203 |
| Fruit and Flowers | 205 |
| A Journalistic Experiment | 207 |
| The Hudson Bay Company | 209 |
| Mr. Brydges | 211 |
| St. Boniface | 213 |
| Archbishop Taché | 215 |
| Advice to Electors | 217 |
| A French Newspaper | 219 |

## CHAPTER X.
### THE PROVINCE OF MANITOBA.

| | PAGE |
|---|---|
| Opinions about the Region | 221 |
| Extent of the Province | 223 |
| Farming in Manitoba | 225 |
| Red River Farmers | 227 |
| Prairie Grasses | 229 |
| Grasshoppers | 231 |
| Manitoba Homesteads | 233 |

## CHAPTER XI.
### MENNONITES AND ICELANDERS IN MANITOBA.

| | |
|---|---|
| Mennonite Homes | 237 |
| Mennonite Doctrines and Habits | 239 |
| Failings of the Mennonites | 241 |
| Mennonite Exclusiveness | 243 |
| New Iceland | 245 |
| Discord among the Icelanders | 247 |

## CHAPTER XII.
### THE NORTH-WEST TERRITORIES.

| | |
|---|---|
| Western Roads | 249 |
| Mudholes | 251 |
| Prairie Hotels | 253 |
| Royal Commissioners in Manitoba | 255 |
| Journalism at Rapid City | 257 |
| Successful Farmers | 259 |
| Home of the Buffalo | 261 |
| Sale of Intoxicants Prohibited | 263 |

## CHAPTER XIII.
### THE CANADIAN FAR WEST.

| | |
|---|---|
| Western Winters | 267 |
| Climate, Soil, and Minerals | 269 |
| Sir George Simpson's Prophecy | 271 |
| Canadian Pacific Railway | 273 |
| Hudson Bay Route | 275 |
| Rival Regions | 277 |
| Perfect Wheat Plants | 279 |
| The "Land of Misery" | 281 |
| A Terrestrial Paradise | 283 |
| Canada's Future | 285 |

## SUPPLEMENTARY CHAPTER.
### WEEDS IN NORTH AMERICA.

| | |
|---|---|
| Weeds in North America | 287 |

## MAPS AND ILLUSTRATIONS.

|   |   |   | PAGE |
|---|---|---|---|
| 1. | MAP OF NEWFOUNDLAND. | . . . . | *Frontispiece* |
| 2. | Do. MANITOBA . | . . . . . . | 233 |
| 3. | Do. DOMINION OF CANADA | . . . . | 295 |
| 4. | WINNIPEG AS IT WAS IN 1870 . | . . . . | 197 |
| 5. | Do. AS IT IS . | . . . . . . | 212 |

# NEWFOUNDLAND TO MANITOBA.

## CHAPTER I.

ENGLAND'S OLDEST COLONY.

### I.

NEWFOUNDLAND was discovered in the reign of Henry the Seventh and incorporated with the English realm in the reign of Queen Elizabeth. It is an Island presenting many and marked contrasts to the Fiji Islands which have been added to the British Empire in the reign of Queen Victoria. In Fiji every prospect pleases and man does the reverse, owing to a taste for eating his fellows. Nature often wears a rude and forbidding aspect in Newfoundland; the aborigines, on the other hand, were too mild and inoffensive to survive the invasion of savage Mic-Mac Indians and the effects of civilized vices imported by white men from Europe.

Money is made in Fiji by growing and crushing sugar-cane; in Newfoundland fortunes have been accumulated by catching and curing fish. The colonists of Fiji are envied for basking in summer weather all the year round, while the Newfoundlanders are pitied for having to sustain a struggle for existence amid the icy gales and fogs of the Northern Atlantic. If the lot of the latter were as sad as is commonly supposed, they would be pardoned for repining and complaining that it was intolerable. Though not more contented than other mortals or reluctant to exercise the truly British prerogative of grumbling, yet their grievances are not those for which Nature can fairly be held responsible. They are proud of their Island despite its fancied drawbacks, loving it with a devotion which nothing can impair. The intensity of a Newfoundlander's patriotism is a striking and admirable trait in his character. His patriotism is evidently as genuine as it is profound. Even new comers soon learn to vie with the native-born inhabitants in extolling the Island's charms. Life in Newfoundland has many compensations and enjoyments which are unsuspected by a stranger.

For many years after the month of June, 1497, when John Cabot discovered this Island, nothing was done by Englishmen to profit by its natural advantages. The earliest notices of it are to be found in the records of Henry the Seventh's privy purse expenses; the first of these references is dated the 10th of August, 1497, and is to the effect that 10*l*. were given "to hym that found the new Isle;" the last is dated 25th August 1505, and is a reward of 13*s*. 4*d*. to Clays for going to Richmond "with wilde catts and popingays of the Newfound Island." Entries between these dates relate to two payments of 20*l*. and one of 30*l*. made to merchants that had voyaged to Newfoundland, and to a reward of 1*l*. "to one that brought hawkes from the New-founded Island." It was not till 1540 that Englishmen sailing from the ports of Biddeford, Barnstable and Bristol systematically engaged in the Newfoundland fisheries. As early as 1504, the Portuguese had begun to catch cod there; fifteen years later, the crews of forty vessels belonging to Portuguese, Spaniards and French-men were thus employed. In 1578, England had 50 vessels, Portugal 50 and France and Spain 150 occupied in reaping the harvest of the sea in the North Atlantic.

The value of Newfoundland as a fishing station having been demonstrated, it was resolved to send colonists thither. The first essay towards carrying out this resolve was made by Mr. Robert

Thorne of Bristol, in 1527; the second, by Mr.
Hore of London, a man whom Hakluyt describes
as "of goodly stature and great courage and
given to the study of Cosmography." Mr. Hore
persuaded many gentlemen and others to join
with him in an undertaking which Henry the
Eighth regarded with approval. The party to
the number of "about six score persons whereof
thirty were gentlemen" embarked at Gravesend,
towards the end of April 1536, in the *Trinity* and
*Minion*. Before embarking, the entire party
"mustered in warlike manner and received the
Sacrament." They returned home in October
after visiting Newfoundland, getting a glimpse of
the natives, observing that the land was covered
with fir and pine trees, undergoing such great
privations through lack of provisions that the
strong killed the weak and ate their flesh. The
survivors took forcible possession of a French
ship and sailed in it to England. It is related
by Hakluyt that Mr. Thomas Buts, one of the
party, "was so changed in the voyage with
hunger and misery" that his father and mother
Sir William and Lady Buts, of Norfolk, "knew
him not to be their son, until they found a secret
mark which was a wart upon one of his knees."

The subsequent action of the French crew,
whom the English had shamefully used, gave

Henry the Eighth an opportunity to display the better side of his character. Hakluyt records that these Frenchmen reached England certain months after "and made complaint to King Henry the Eighth: the King causing the matter to be examined, and finding the great distress of his subjects, and the causes of the dealing so with the French, was so moved with pity, that he punished not his subjects, but of his own purse made full and royal recompense unto the French."[1]

The most detailed account of Newfoundland as it appeared to the early visitors is contained in a letter of Mr. Anthony Parkhurst of Bristol to Mr. Richard Hakluyt of the Middle Temple, dated 13th of November 1578. Parkhurst had made several voyages to the Island, and Hakluyt having applied to him for information, Parkhurst said in reply that he hoped Hakluyt would use his influence to induce men in power to help in christianizing Newfoundland or rather, as he phrases it, "to redeem the people of Newfoundland and those parts from out of the captivity of that spiritual Pharaoh, the devil." He gives a glowing picture of the Island. He says that the soil is good and fertile, that, in sundry places, he had " sown wheat, barley, rye, oats, beans, peas,

---

[1] Hakluyt's Works, ed. 1810, vol. 3, pp. 168—170.

and seeds of herbs, kernels, plumstones, nuts, all of which have prospered as in England. The country yieldeth many good trees of fruit, as filberts in some places, but in all places cherry trees, and a kind of pear tree meet to graft on. As for roses they are as common as brambles here; strawberries, dewberries and raspberries, as common as grass. The timber is most fir, yet plenty of pineapple trees; few of these two kinds meet to mast a ship of three score and ten [tons]; but near Cape Breton, and to the Southward, big and sufficient for any ship. There be also oaks and thorns, there is in all the country plenty of birch and alder, which be the meetest wood for cold, and also willow, which will serve for any other purposes. As touching the kinds of fish beside cod, there are herrings, salmons, thornebacke, plaice, or rather we should call them flounders, dog fish, and another most excellent of taste called by us a cat, oysters and muscles, in which I have found pearls above forty in one muscle, and generally all have some, great or small. I heard of a Portugal that found one worth 300 ducats. There are also other kinds of shell fish, as limpets, cockles, wilks, lobsters and crabs; also a fish like a smelt which cometh on shore, and another that hath the like property, called a squid." He calls the climate temperate and far pleasanter than might be supposed from the tales of "foolish mariners." He depicts the land as being intersected with rivers and covered

in places with lakes full of fish: "There are
plenty of bears everywhere, so that you may kill
of them as oft as you list; their flesh is as good
as young beef, and hardly you may know the one
from the other if it be powdered but two days.
Of otters we may take like store. There are sea-
gulls, murres, ducks, wild geese, and many other
kind of birds store, too long to write, especially
at one island named Penguin, where we may drive
them on a plank into our ship, as many as shall
lade her." Deer, hares, foxes and wolves
abounded. In addition to possessing a fruitful
soil, and many varieties of trees, animals and fish,
the Island was believed by Parkhurst to be
rich in minerals; he had found and brought
home with him specimens of iron and copper
ore.

The foregoing particulars, which Parkhurst
communicated to Hakluyt, were doubtless known
to many persons and increased their desire to
colonize the Island. In the year that Parkhurst's
letter was written, Sir Humphrey Gilbert procured Letters Patent from Queen Elizabeth authorizing him to search for and occupy unknown
lands or places which were not in the occupation
of the subjects of any Christian potentate. In
those days, as at a later time, the natives of a
country whose skins were dark and who had
never heard of Christ, were denied any rights

which white-faced Christians were bound to respect. The Christians considered themselves justified in taking possession of the lands of these heathen barbarians on the plea that they would teach them to read the Bible and rescue them from the dominion of Satan.

Sir Humphrey Gilbert's first attempt at exploration failed after he had collected a fleet and persuaded many persons to join him. He returned to England without accomplishing anything, and with the loss of a vessel. Sir Walter Raleigh, his half-brother, who was associated with him in the enterprise, was to have accompanied him when he set out the second time, from Causet bay near Plymouth, on the 11th of June 1583; but Raleigh did not go and the vessel which he had fitted out put back to port shortly after sailing. However, Raleigh sent a letter to Sir Humphrey Gilbert, immediately before the latter sailed, containing a message from Queen Elizabeth to the effect that she wished him "as great good hap and safety to his ship as if she herself were there in person," this letter being accompanied with a jewel from the Queen in the form of an anchor guided by a lady. A narrative of the expedition has been written by Captain Hayes, one of the few survivors. He says the fleet consisted of five vessels, the *Delight*, 120 tons burden, the *Raleigh*

200 tons, the *Golden Hind* 40 tons, the *Swallow* 40 tons, and the *Squirrel* 10 tons. The party numbered about 260, " among whom we had of every faculty good choice, as shipwrights, masons, carpenters, smiths and such like, requisite to such an action; also mineral men and refiners. Besides, for solace of our people, and allurements of the savages, we were provided of music in good variety: not omitting the least toys, as morris dancers, hobby horses and Maylike conceits to delight the savage people, whom we intended to win by all fair means possible. And to that end we were indifferently furnished of all pretty haberdashery wares to barter with those simple people."

Their first mischance, as has been stated, was that the *Raleigh* parted company soon after sailing, and put back; their second was that the crew of the *Swallow* engaged in piracy. However, they reached the harbour of St. Johns, Newfoundland on the 3rd of August. The next day being Sunday, Sir Humphrey and his company went on shore under the escort of the English merchants, " who showed us their accustomed walks unto a place they call the Garden. But nothing appeared more than Nature itself without art, who confusedly hath brought forth roses abundantly, wild, but odoriferous and to sense very comfortable. Also the like plenty of raspberries, which do grow in every place." On the following day, Sir Humphrey Gilbert read his Letters Patent and took possession of the country in the Queen's name. A fortnight was spent in exploring the country and in trying to communicate with the aborigines. It was found that there were no natives in the Southern part, and it was supposed that this arose from the south coast "being so much frequented by Christians." In the Northern part they found savages who were "altogether harmless."

The country pleased them. They liked the climate; they were struck with the abundance of fish and game and with the fine flowers which grew luxuriantly. Indeed, Captain Hayes expresses his thankfulness to God for having superabundantly replenished the earth with creatures for the use of man, though man hath not used a fifth part of the same, and this consideration, in his opinion, "doth aggravate the fault and foolish sloth in many of our nation, choosing rather to live indirectly, and very miserably to live and die within this realm pestered with inhabitants, than to adventure as becometh men, to obtain a habitation in those remote lands, in which Nature very prodigally doth minister unto men's endeavours, and for art to work upon." Captain Hayes notes that there are traces of minerals in many places, that iron is plentiful, and that lead

and copper are to be met with. Sir Humphrey
Gilbert's avowed desire was to discover silver or
gold. "Amongst other charges given to inquire
out the singularities of this country, the General
(Sir Humphrey) was most curious in the search
of metals, commanding the mineral man and
refiner, especially to be diligent. The same was
a Saxon born, honest and religious, named Daniel,
who after search brought at first some sort of ore,
seeming rather to be iron than other metal. The
next time he found ore, which with no small show
of contentment he delivered unto the General,
using protestation, that if silver were the thing
which might satisfy the General and his followers,
there it was, advising him to seek no further: the
peril whereof he undertook upon his life (as dear
unto him as the Crown of England unto her
Majesty, that I may use his own words) if it fell
not out accordingly." Captain Hayes avows that
he was sceptical about the value of the "mineral
man's" discovery, and adds Sir Humphrey
was so thoroughly satisfied that he took precautions to keep the discovery a secret lest the
Portuguese and French, who were in force there,
might seize the *Delight* freighted with the precious
ore. The *Delight* was lost soon after on Sable
Island, the island on which the Cunard steamer
*Britannia* grounded for a short time when Charles
Dickens crossed the Atlantic in 1842. A man of
letters, who was a passenger on board the *Delight*,

perished when that vessel was wrecked. This was Stephanus Parmenius, a learned Hungarian who, in the language of Captain Hayes, " of piety and zeal to good attempts, adventured in this action, minding to record in the Latin tongue, the gests and things worthy of remembrance, happening in this discovery, to the honour of our nation, the same being adorned with the eloquent style of this orator and rare poet of our time." The only record of the voyage, which this learned Hungarian has left, is a Latin epistle written at St. Johns and addressed to Hakluyt who has turned it into English. What impressed Parmenius the most was the incredible abundance of fish, " whereby great gain grows to them that travel to these parts: the hook is no sooner thrown out, but it is eftsoones drawn up with some goodly fish: the whole land is full of hills and woods. The trees for the most part are pines and of them some are very old, and some young: a great part of them being fallen by reason of their age, doth so hinder the sight of the land, and stop the way of those that seek to travel, that they can go no whither: all the grass here is long and tall, and little differeth from ours. It seemeth also that the nature of this soil is fit for corn: for I found certain blades and ears in a manner bearded, so that it appeareth that by manuring and sowing, they may easily be framed for the use of man: here are in the woods bush berries or rather strawberries, growing up like trees, of great sweetness. Bears also appear about the fishers' stages of the country, and are sometimes killed, but they seem to be white, as I conjectured by their skins, and somewhat less than ours."

Another passenger whose loss was even more lamented was Daniel, " our Saxon refiner and discoverer of inestimable riches." Sir Humphrey Gilbert deeply mourned the loss of Daniel and of the ore on board the *Delight* as well as of his own notes and books. The discovery of ore had altered his opinion as regards Newfoundland and he intimated that, whereas he previously had a great predilection for the southern part of the North American Continent, now he was wholly in favour of the northern. Had he been spared, it is probable that the colonization of Virginia might not have taken place for a longer space of time. The failure of his expedition to Newfoundland directed all the thoughts and efforts of Sir Walter Raleigh and others towards effecting the settlement of Virginia. Sir Humphrey's confidence was so extreme that he believed he could persuade Queen Elizabeth to lend him 10,000*l*. wherewith to prosecute his enterprise the following spring. His hopes were destined to die with him and that speedily.

Sir Humphrey Gilbert's death is one of the tragic episodes in the annals of adventure. He resolved to sail home in the *Squirrel* a cockle shell of 10 tons. He was entreated to leave that vessel and take passage in the *Golden Hind*, being urged to make the exchange on the ground that he ran great risk by remaining in the *Squirrel*. His admirable reply was " I will not forsake my little company going homeward, with whom I have passed so many storms and perils." Soon after he had thus spoken the wind blew a gale and the sea raged tumultuously so that both vessels were in extreme peril. On the afternoon of Monday the 9th of September 1583, the *Squirrel* nearly foundered, but the vessel recovering, Sir Humphrey was seen by those in the *Golden Hind* seated on the deck with a book in his hand, and he was heard exclaiming, whenever the vessels approached within speaking distance of each other, "we are as near to heaven by sea as by land." Captain Hayes adds: "The same Monday night, about 12 of the clock, or not long after, the *Squirrel* being ahead of us in the *Golden Hind*, suddenly her lights were out, whereof as it were in a moment, we lost the sight, and withal our watch cryed, the General was cast away, which was too true."

The tangible result of Sir Humphrey Gilbert's expedition was the formal addition of Newfoundland to the English realm. After he had read his Letters Patent; "had delivered unto him (after the custom of England) a rod and a turf of soil," set up the arms of England, engraved on lead, in a conspicuous place, there could be no dispute as to which European State had professed to have taken possession of the Island. He followed the ceremony of taking possession with an act of legislation, promulgating three Laws which were to take immediate effect, the first ordaining that the public exercise of religion should be after the pattern of the Church of England; the second enjoining the pains and penalties of high treason against the persons who should question or attack the Queen's title to the country; the third providing that "if any person shall utter words sounding to the dishonour of her Majesty, he should lose his ears, and have his ship and goods confiscate."

Captain Richard Whitbourne, the author of the first book written about Newfoundland, was present on this occasion. He confirms the reports of other observers as to the fruitfulness of the land. Fruits, flowers and herbs he saw growing in great profusion; moreover, there was "great store of deer's flesh in that country, and no want of good fish, good fowl, good fresh water, and store of wood. By which commodities people may live very pleasantly." He argued with great show of reason that such a country was well adapted for settlement. He held, not only that people could make new and comfortable homes for themselves there, but also "that by a plantation there and by that means only, the poor mis-believing inhabitants of that country may be reduced from barbarism to the knowledge of God and the light of his truth, and to a civil and regular kind of life and government."

Both Captain Hayes and Captain Whitbourne saw strange monsters during their visits to Newfoundland. The latter minutely describes an animal which he fancies to be a merman or mermaid, but which was probably a seal. The former thus describes a monster which bears a resemblance to that represented in the accounts of the sea serpent: "Upon Saturday in the afternoon the 31st of August [1583] we changed our course, and returned back for England, at which very instant, even in winding about, there passed along between us and towards the land which we now forsook a very lion to our seeming, in shape, hair and colour, not swimming after the manner of a beast by moving of his feet, but rather sliding upon the water with his whole body (excepting the legs) in sight, neither yet diving under, and again rising above the water, as the manner is,

of whales, dolphins, tunnies, porpoises and other
fish; but confidently showing himself above water
without hiding, notwithstanding we presented
ourselves in open view and gesture to amaze him,
as all creatures will be commonly at a sudden
gaze and sight of men. Thus he passed along
turning his head to and fro, yawning and gaping
wide, with ugly demonstration of long teeth, and
glaring eyes, and to bid us a farewell (coming
right against the *Hind*) he sent forth a horrible
voice, roaring and bellowing as doth a lion, which
spectacle we all beheld so far as we were able to
discern the same, as men prone to wonder at
every strange thing, as this doubtless was, to see
a lion in the Ocean sea, or fish in shape of a
lion."[2]

The colonization of Newfoundland was one of
Bacon's favourite projects; he believed that the
country was well suited for settlement and that
the surrounding sea contained even more precious
treasure than that which was embedded in the
mountains of Mexico and Peru. He was a
partner in a company which obtained an extensive grant of land in Newfoundland from James
the First, and John Guy, a merchant of Bristol,
was sent forth to found a colony at Conception
Bay. He sailed from Bristol in 1610 with
three ships filled with emigrants, established

---

[2] Hakluyt, vol. 3, p. 200.

himself and his followers at the appointed place
and opened up an intercourse with the Indians.
For some unexplained reason many of the colonists determined to return home, which they did
in 1612. Eleven years later Sir George Calvert
obtained a large grant of land from the King
which he styled the Province of Avalon. Here
he built himself a house and settled with his
family and several followers. A French settlement had been made not far distant and the rival
settlers were on terms of enmity. Sir George
Calvert built a fort to protect his settlement from
the attacks of the French; he became tired, however, of the hostilities which he had to wage and
returned with his family to England. He received from Charles the First a grant of land on
the American Continent where he founded a
highly successful colony, the land itself being now
known as the State of Maryland. Lord Falkland
sent a few colonists to Newfoundland from Ireland in 1628 and a few more went from England
under the supervision of Sir David Kirk in 1654
and with the sanction of the Parliament.

Charles the First considered it his duty to issue
a code of laws to govern the Newfoundland
fishermen. According to this code any person
accused of murder or theft of articles valued
at 40 shillings was to be brought to England for

trial; all persons were prohibited from casting ballast into harbours or destroying the stages used in drying and curing fish; it was ordered that, according to ancient custom, the master of the ship which first entered the harbour at the beginning of the fishery should be Admiral, and exercise jurisdiction over the others and enjoy special privileges; all persons were forbidden to deface or alter the distinguishing marks on boats, to purloin salt or other provision belonging to the fishing trade, to set fire to the woods of the country or work detriment to them by "rinding of the trees," to cast anchor where the hauling of bait might be hindered, to rob the nets of others, or take bait out of their boats and, lastly, it was enjoined that the ships' companies should assemble on Sundays and hear Divine service read to them, the prayers to be "such as are in the Book of Common Prayer." In this summary of the laws which Charles issued, I have omitted the tenth Clause of the Commission which is in some respects the most noteworthy, being one of the earliest attempts made to suppress the sale not only of strong drink but also of tobacco. Its terms are: "That no person do set up any tavern for selling of wine, beer, or strong waters, cyder or tobacco, to entertain the fishermen; because it is found that by such means they are debauched, neglecting their labour, and poor ill-governed men not only spend most part of their *shares* before they come home upon which the life and maintenance of their wives and children depend, but are likewise hurtful in divers other ways, as, by neglecting and making themselves unfit for their labour, by purloining and stealing from their owners, and making unlawful shifts to supply their disorders, which disorders they frequently follow since these occasions have presented themselves."

Two hundred years elapsed after Charles the First gave these laws to Newfoundland before the people of the Island exercised the right of legislating for themselves. In that long interval the Islanders were treated as children who did not know what was good for them and their Island was regarded as nothing more than a fishing station. Indeed, the utmost efforts were used to prevent its becoming anything else. The wish of any person to settle and till the soil was thwarted in every possible way. The masters of vessels were strictly prohibited from carrying any settlers thither. It was supposed that, if the Island were covered with persons engaged in farming or cattle rearing, the fisheries would be neglected. This dread led to the issuing of the most iniquitous decree for which the Government of any civilized community can be held responsible. At the instance, as was supposed, of Sir Josiah Child, a London merchant, a man accounted far more enlightened than his contemporaries and one of the earliest writers on Political Economy, the Government of Charles the Second decreed the destruction of the colony, Sir John Berry being commissioned to burn down the houses in order that the settlers might be compelled to depart. This inhuman edict was modified through the representations made to the King by John Downing, a settler; his Majesty being graciously pleased to command that the houses were to be allowed to remain. However, rigid steps were taken for hindering any person residing on the Island who was not directly engaged in the fisheries.

Down to the year 1811, no house could be erected on the Island without the written permission of the Governor. Letters are extant showing that the Governors ordered the demolition of houses erected there without their consent and also that they forbade the cultivation of the soil. The following example of this almost incredible policy is to be found in a letter written in October, 1790, by Governor Milbanke to George Hutchins: "I have considered your request respecting the alteration which you wish to make in your storehouse near the waterside, and as it appears that the alteration will not be in any ways injurious to the fishery, you have hereby permission to make it. As to Alexander Long's house, which has been built contrary to his Majesty's express commands, made known to the inhabitants of this place by my proclamation of the 13th of last October, it must and shall come down. . . . . I shall embrace this opportunity of warning you against making an improper use of any other part of (what you are pleased to call) your ground, for you may rest assured that every house or other building erected upon it hereafter, without the permission—in writing—of the Governor for the time being—except such building and erection as shall be actually on purpose for the curing, salting, drying and husbanding of fish . . must unavoidably be taken down and removed, in obedience to his Majesty's said commands. And it may not be amiss at the same time to inform you, I am also directed not to allow any possession as private property to be taken of, or any right of property whatever to be acknowledged in any land whatever which is not actually employed in the fishery."

The conduct of Governor Milbanke was not exceptional; his successor Governor Waldegrave wrote in the same strain and acted in the same style. In a letter addressed to the sheriff in 1797, he says: " Your having suffered Thomas Nevan to put up what you are pleased to call a few sheds, is clearly an infraction of my orders;

you will therefore direct him to remove them
immediately; which, if not complied with, I desire
that you will yourself see this order executed.
You will take good care that Jeremiah Marroty
and John Fitzgerald do not erect chimneys to
their sheds, or even light fires in them of any
kind." The parental despotism which interfered
with the building of houses and the construction
of chimneys naturally extended to the prices of
provisions. Thus, Governor Edwards having
issued a decree that the price of beef, veal and
mutton was to be 1s. per lb. and Luke Ryan
having sold beef at 1s. 3d. a lb., the latter was
fined 10l. for his offence. The boatkeepers at
Harbour Grace, having complained of the merchants charging too much for provisions, the
Governor ordered that the prices charged there
should be the same as at St. Johns, notwithstanding that the extra carriage to Harbour Grace
necessitated the imposition of a higher charge in
order to reap a profit corresponding to that obtained at St. Johns. Governor Waldegrave
recognized the fact that the fishermen had a
hard struggle for subsistence. He describes the
fishermen, in a letter to the Duke of Portland, as
" a set of unfortunate beings, working like slaves,
and hazarding their lives, when, at the expiration
of their term (however successful their exertions),
they find themselves not only without gain, but so

deeply indebted as forces them to emigrate, or drives them to despair." The foregoing remarks on the condition of the fishermen were elicited by a remonstrance from the merchants against the fishermen at Burin being suffered to emigrate. Many instances occur in the history of Newfoundland which prompt the inquiry whether an essential difference existed between the relation of the fishermen to the merchants in that Island and that of the slaves to their masters in the West India Islands and the Southern States of the Union?

The picture given of the condition of Newfoundland at the end of the last century is not a pleasing one. The poorer classes were in great suffering and were naturally discontented with their hard lot. The richer classes displayed, according to Governor Waldegrave, "an insolent idea of independence (which will some day show itself more forcibly) and a firm resolution to oppose every measure of government which a Governor may think proper to propose for the general benefit of the Island." One of the reasons which made him think so was the refusal of the merchants to submit to taxation. The consumption of rum having increased to a great extent, the Governor estimated that a tax of sixpence a gallon levied upon the rum imported would defray the entire cost of the Government and that it would be fairer to do this than to call upon the Mother Country to bear the burden. When the merchants were sounded on the subject, they expressed their sentiments in a letter which is a curiosity in its way. They stated that they would be "extremely concerned to see any species of taxes introduced into this Island, which would inevitably be burdensome and inconvenient to the trade and fishery in general, and we trust that in the wisdom of his Majesty's Ministers, no such innovation will take place." During his Administration an attempt was made to provide relief for the destitute, a fund being formed for the purpose by voluntary subscription. That plan afterwards gave place to a regular system of charity from funds raised by taxation. The demand for relief has gone on increasing at so rapid a rate as to suggest that something must be seriously wrong in the system which leads to such a result. Two generations after the introduction of the palliative which Governor Waldegrave devised for the succour of the destitute, one-third of the public expenditure of the Colony was absorbed in pauper relief.

The retention of the fisheries on the Banks of Newfoundland in British hands was for many years the great object of British statesmen. The elder Pitt, in one of his impassioned speeches, declared those fisheries to be so valuable to the country that they must be preserved even though foreign soldiers had captured the Tower of London. Whatever tended to promote the fisheries was favourably regarded by the British Government, while any scheme for benefiting the people of Newfoundland was either regarded with indifference or rejected as inopportune. In consequence of this the Islanders made but little progress; their numbers were comparatively small; the fixed population of the Island did not much exceed 10,000 at the beginning of the present century. During the winter season, when the fishery was over, it was deemed appropriate that the Governor should leave the Island. It was not till 1818 that Governor Pickmore broke through the established rule and lived there all the year round. Since then the Governor finds plenty to occupy himself in winter as well as in summer, and the office itself has not only risen in dignity, but has also been illustrated by men of great capacity and distinction.

The slowness with which this Colony made its way to the position which it now occupies cannot be better exemplified than by the fact that, not till 1807, was a newspaper published there. Its modern history dates from 1855 when responsible

Government was granted. Twenty-two years earlier a Representative Assembly was constituted. It is since the Colony has been truly self-governing, that its progress has been most marked, and that its dissensions have become less serious and violent. Although a large part of the people from the earliest days belonged to the Church of Rome, it was not till 1784 that a Roman Catholic priest was permitted to discharge in public the duties of his sacred calling. Till 1875, the subject of religious teaching in public schools was a constant source of discussion and bitterness. No system of general education meeting with approval, the young were prevented from having a fair start in life. Now, however, there is a national system of education based on the plan of dividing the fund voted by the Legislative Assembly among the several bodies in proportion to their numbers, and thus the chief step has been taken to ensure that future generations of Newfoundlanders will be wiser than their progenitors. Other changes and movements in the path of progress will be noted hereafter.

## II.

Though St. Johns, the Capital of Newfoundland, is about 1000 miles nearer the United Kingdom than

New York, the means of communication are greater between Liverpool and New York than between Liverpool and St. Johns. An Allan steamer runs direct between Newfoundland and the United Kingdom every fortnight during nine months in the year, while passengers and letters are conveyed by way of Halifax during the other three months. If the Government of Newfoundland did not pay the Allan Company a subsidy of 12,000*l.* the facilities for passing from the Island of Great Britain to the Island of Newfoundland would be even less than they are, while the postal arrangements would be as primitive as in the days of Queen Elizabeth. This constitutes one of the grievances, referred to at the outset, which gives the Islanders greater concern than the climate. It is held by them that the Mother Country ought at least to contribute something towards the mail service between the two Islands.

I visited Newfoundland in the Allan liner *Caspian*, under the command of Captain Trocks, an experienced sailor and excellent man. The *Caspian* is one of three steamers which ply between Liverpool and Baltimore, touching at St. Johns and Halifax. Two thirds of my fellow-passengers were Newfoundlanders, all of whom were firmly of opinion that St. Johns was a city second to none, that the climate of the Island was unequalled for salubrity and that the Island was as nearly perfect as any other spot on the earth's surface. When it was suggested that improvements might be possible, that the interior of the Island should be thoroughly explored, that its agricultural and mineral resources could be better developed, and that railways might prove of great service in these respects, some of them scouted the very notion as superlatively absurd. It seems natural for Newfoundland to form part of the Dominion of Canada; yet, when union was proposed, the opposition in the Island was overwhelming. Mr. Bennett, the Premier at that time, looked upon the scheme with genuine horror, and he laboured with mortifying success to convince his prejudiced fellows that Confederation would be succeeded by increased taxation, their virtual enslavement and utter ruin. Many men have prospered exceedingly under the existing Government in Newfoundland and they are apprehensive of the effects of any change and indisposed to hasten it. The rich merchants apparently consider that everything has been ordered for the best in the best of all islands, whilst the poor are too ignorant to appreciate the changes which would prove beneficial and too inert to agitate for them. If money and knowledge were more equally disseminated the aversion to new things and ideas would be less, while the desire to know more about the Island itself, and contribute towards its farther development would be far greater. Extraordinary though the statement may seem, it is literally true that the interior of Newfoundland, especially towards the northern side, is as undeveloped a region as the middle of Greenland, and the heart of Africa.

When the weather is propitious the approach to the Island impresses every admirer of grand scenery. I was told that the spectacle was striking; the reality exceeded my anticipations. On either hand, as far as the eye can reach, the rocks which rise from the sea to the height of several hundred feet, are moulded into fantastic forms by the incessant dashing against them of the Atlantic waves. The masses of floating ice play a part in affecting the appearance of the rocks. Navigation in the spring is rendered hazardous here owing to icebergs and fields of ice. As the *Caspian* nears the land it is difficult to understand where the entrance occurs into the famous harbour of St. Johns; it is not till the steamer is comparatively close in shore that a breach is seen in the rock bound coast, which is 220 fathoms wide at the inlet, and 95 at the opposite end of the Narrows where the harbour is reached, this harbour being a sheet of land-locked deep water, a mile and a quarter long and one-third of a mile wide. With the exception of Halifax, there is no finer harbour in this region of the world. In former days it was hard for a ship to run the gauntlet of forts which command the Narrows. If the old fortifications were repaired and put into a proper state of defence no hostile force could pass or take them. St Johns has not inaptly been styled the Gibraltar of the Atlantic.

The capital of Newfoundland is situated on the slope of a hill. Its population at the time of the last census was 30,574. This was in 1874, and and it showed an increase over the census taken in 1869 of seventeen hundred persons. As there is much building going on, it may be assumed that the population of St Johns is increasing at a satisfactory rate. Though founded so long ago as the year 1572, the city has none of the marks of age. This modern look is due to the fact that the houses are all of recent date, having been erected within the last 30 years. More than once the entire city has been swept away by fire, and the last time this occurred the impression made was so profound that proper precautions are now observed to hinder a recurrence of the like calamity. In the lower streets, where an outbreak of fire would be most serious, as the flames would spread from them to the buildings in the upper streets, the erection of wooden structures is absolutely prohibited. Moreover an ample service of water, always available, has been provided for the extinction of a fire in any part of the city. At the water's level there are wharves which run round the Bay. They are lined with stores in which the process of extracting oil from seals is carried on, and with warehouses in which cod are packed for exportation. Behind the wharves on the North side is Water Street, about a mile and a half long, wherein are the principal shops and merchant's warehouses, the post-office and the Custom House. This street has the uninviting aspect of similar streets in seaport towns, the services of a scavenger being obviously required. The other streets are cleaner and they contain many neat houses of brick or wood.

The most conspicuous edifice in St. Johns, when approached from the sea, is the Roman Catholic Cathedral. It is built of stone; its form is that of a Latin cross; its extreme length is 237 feet; it has two towers which rise to the height of 138 feet. Internally it is richly ornamented. Close at hand the Church of England Cathedral is now in course of erection from the design of the late Sir Gilbert Scott. Its length is 120 feet, its width is 56 feet and its tower and spire are to be 130 feet high. The nave was finished and opened for divine service in 1852. At that time the cost was $200,000, and at least another $100,000 must be expended before the building is finished. When complete in all its parts, this Cathedral will be one of the grandest piles on this side of the Atlantic. There are other churches belonging either to the Roman Catholics or to members of the Church of England. The Wesleyan Methodists possess more than one church, and the Presbyterians who, though small in number, abound in intellect and wealth, have recently erected a very tasteful stone Church at a cost of $50,000. Among the public buildings which attract a stranger's notice is the Athenæum, where lectures and concerts take place, and which has a library and reading-room for the use of the members; it is the property of a company and it is so admirably managed as to yield a dividend to its proprietors. St. Patrick's Hall, a more recent structure, is also used for public meetings. No public building is so noticeable at night as the Custom House owing to the large red light which shines from the upper part and serves as a beacon to vessels passing through the Narrows into the Bay.

The Colonial Building or Parliament House

and the Government House are the two largest public buildings. They are situate on the plateau which stretches for some distance inland from the upper part of the city. The view of the surrounding country is not unlike that from the elevated ground in South Devon and far more picturesque than that which the stranger expects to find in an Island which has been depicted as barren and unattractive. The eye gazes upon cultivated fields, clumps of trees, villas encompassed with gardens. The Colonial Building is surrounded by balsam poplars. The building is of white limestone imported from Cork; it has a stone portico supported by pillars, the front resembling that of the British Museum in its general outline. In this Building the staff of some of the government departments is accommodated as well as the Legislative Assembly when that body is in session. The Upper House or Legislative Council numbers 15, the Lower one, or House of Assembly numbers 31. The rule in the British House of Commons is not observed in the Newfoundland House of Assembly, as to the relative positions of the Ministry and the Opposition. At present the Newfoundland Opposition occupy seats to the right of the Speaker and the Ministry to the left. The Ministry may sit on either side; the other members keep their seats irrespective of a change of Government. But the most comfortable seats are on the Speaker's left because a large fireplace is at that side of the Chamber. In Newfoundland politics, the party farther from the fire is the one which experiences the "Cold shade of Opposition." The acoustic properties of the Chamber are very bad owing, possibly, to the great height of the ceiling and to the intercepting effect of a large chandelier. As it was found that the reporters of the Press could not hear the debates in the gallery set apart for for them at the end opposite to the Speaker, seats have been provided for them close to his chair, the members of the Assembly thinking it better that reporters should be admitted to the body of the Chamber than that their speeches should be unrecorded. The qualification for a seat in either House of Legislature is the possession of an income not less than $400 or of property to the nett value of $2000. Every male person who has attained the age of 21 years and has occupied a dwelling-house for a year as tenant or proprietor is an elector. Votes are recorded openly in the old English fashion.

The party lines were drawn between Protestants and Roman Catholics and, strange though it may seem, the Protestants being styled Conservatives, and the Roman Catholics, Liberals. It would have surprised the late Pope Pius the Ninth, who execrated the very epithet Liberal, to have learned that his devout adherents in Newfoundland gloried in applying it to each other. Happily, the days of bitter religious disputes have passed away in this Island. I have already stated that the question of appropriating the fund for educating the people which was the chief subject of contention and source of animosity has been amicably adjusted by dividing the fund among the several religious denominations. Another question which also caused strife and ill-feeling, the right to control the burying-grounds, has been harmoniously settled by each body having provided for itself a place for burying the dead. I noted a novelty in funerals; this consisted in the coffin, which was borne exposed to sight on a vehicle shaped like a cart, being painted light blue.

Government House divides with the Colonial Building the honour of being the most important in the Island. It is one of the plain stone buildings which Mr. Ruskin has characterized and denounced as huge boxes with holes in their sides, but which, though deficient in architectural beauty, are not lacking in comfort. The grounds about it are extensive and well laid out. Sir John Glover, the present occupant is one of the best

Governors which the Colony has had; he has taken great pains to make himself acquainted with the scenery and resources of the Island; he has outstripped his predecessors in this respect and no native has a stronger faith than his as to its future capabilities. It is pleasant to be able to add that he enjoys the popularity among all classes which he richly merits. Before passing from these official buildings, I may state that the house of Sir William Whiteway, the present Prime Minister, which is not far distant from them, has a garden attached to it which charmed me greatly. I was struck with the number and beauty of the flowers in all the private gardens, but this one impressed me the most. Among other familiar English flowers, I saw dahlias in fine condition and looking as if the climate agreed with them. The condition of the gardens was a strong testimony not only to the care bestowed upon them, but also to the excellence of the climate.

That the soil and climate of Newfoundland are really good is a statement which may be read with scepticism. The common opinion is unfavourable to both, and this opinion is based upon experience gained near the coast. It is a transparent absurdity to take the climate of Paris as representing that of all France, to suppose that the fogs which sometimes visit London spread on all England, to maintain that the weather which prevails in the city of New York is the same as that prevailing in San Francisco, and to fancy Berlin, the capital of the German empire, enjoying the natural advantages which have made the vine-clad slopes of the Rhine things of beauty and sources of wealth. Newfoundland is not very large, yet it is large enough to have a varied climate and a diversified soil. The Island is nearly the same size as England; its extreme length is 419 miles and, at the widest part its width is about 300 ; its coast-line extends over 2000 miles and its surface over 40,000,000. Mr. W. E. Cormack who traversed the Island from East to West in 1822, being the first white man who did so, has left a vivid picture of what he saw after he had penetrated the dense forest which intercepted his path westward and when standing on an eminence, he obtained a view of the interior : " What a contrast did this present to the conjectures entertained of Newfoundland ! The hitherto mysterious interior lay unfolded upon us—a boundless scene—emerald surface—a vast basin. The eye strides again and again over a succession of northerly and southerly ranges of green plains, marbled with woods and lakes of every form and extent, a picture of all the luxurious scenes of national cultivation receding into invisibleness. . . The great external features of the eastern portion of the main body of the Island are seen from these commanding heights. Overland communication between the bays of the east, north and south Coasts, it appears, might easily be established. . . We descended into the bosom of the interior. The plains which shone so brilliantly are steppes or savannas, composed of fine black compact peat mould, formed by the growth and decay of mosses. They are in the form of extensive gently undulating beds, stretching northward and southward, with running waters and lakes, skirted with woods, lying between them. Their yellow green surfaces are sometimes uninterrupted by either tree, shrub, rock, or any irregularity, for more than ten miles. They are chequered everywhere upon the surface by deep beaten deer paths and are in reality magnificent natural deer parks, adorned with wood and water."

Not till a few years ago was it determined to open up the interior of the Island by constructing a railway across it. A preliminary survey was made in 1868 at the instance and cost of Mr. Sandford Fleming, the eminent Canadian Engineer. In 1875, the Legislature passed an Act for a more extended survey. The reports of the Engineers confirmed all that had been previously written in praise of the Island, while showing how easily it was to construct railways there. Nearly the whole of the interior is undulating, is covered in parts with forest, is intersected with rivers and is strewn with lakes. One third is water. The greater part of the soil is adapted for the growth of all kinds of vegetables, most kinds of grain and even tobacco. On the western side the soil is richer and the climate is finer than in the peninsula of Avalon at the East. If the earliest settlement had taken place at the western shore the Island might now sustain a large population, living by the pursuit of agriculture alone.

Mr. Alexander Murray, the Government Geologist of Newfoundland, has carefully analyzed and summarized the reports of the railway engineers. This summary is the more valuable and instructive because Mr. Murray is personally acquainted with a large portion of the ground passed over and able to estimate the statements made regarding it. He says, with regard to St. George's Bay on the west side, that it forms a convenient harbour and terminus for the trade of the adjacent mineral region. Twenty miles from the harbour there is a coal-field thirty miles long and ten miles broad. "That the Geological character of the country over a vast area, extended to the northward of Bonne Bay, gives promise of the presence of metallic ores, seems well assured ; that the Humber Valley contains marbles of nearly every shade of colour—some of the saccharine variety vieing in purity with the far-famed statuary of Carrara—is well known, and, finally, that there is nothing less than 1000 square miles of country—

including the Humber Valley—scattered over the
region, in every respect worthy of being reclaimed,
I re-assert with confidence. . . As regards climate
and the possibilities of agriculture being properly
pursued, Newfoundland is not, by any means, so
bad as has often been represented. True indeed
it is that the eastern sea-board and this (St.
Johns) immediate part of it, in particular, suffers
much from the effects of the cold arctic currents
which, ice-laden, pass along their shores; but
even here in St. Johns the drawbacks of a late
spring are greatly compensated by the unusually
long continuance of fine weather in the Fall,
which allows barley and oats to ripen well as late
as the middle or end of October; and if we may
be allowed to judge from the experience of those
who have spent much time in the interior (among
whom I am one) the rigours of the coast are to a
great extent modified there, and fogs are exceedingly rare. . . Everyone, nowadays, appears ready
to admit that the Bay of Notre Dame is destined
to develope itself into a great mining region.
Supposing, then, that there were some half a
dozen such establishments as Tilt Cove and Betts
Cove in Notre Dame Bay, the mining population
alone would amount to many thousands of souls,
to say nothing of horses, cattle and the like. . .
There are, beyond all doubt, many places border-
ing on the great Bay of Notre Dame where oats
and barley, turnips and potatoes can be cultivated
as well as in any part of Nova Scotia and grass
crops can be raised as well, if not better, as in
the most favoured regions of the Dominion."

After exhaustive debates in the Newfoundland Legislature and acrimonious discussion in the Press an Act was passed on the 18th of April 1880 authorizing the construction of a narrow-guage railway across the Island with branches to the more important points at a total cost of $5,000,000. The ground upon which this legislative enactment are based may be found in a Report of the Joint Committee of the Legislative Council and Assembly. That Report sets forth that the future of the growing population of the Island is a matter of grave solicitude; that, though the yield of the fisheries has increased, this has not been in proportion to the increase in the population; that it has been proved how much can be gained by a further development of mining and agriculture, the mining industry having been very profitable and the most prosperous of the labouring people being the cultivators of land in the vicinity of St. Johns where the conditions of fertility are far inferior to those in the interior and the Western side of the Island; that, if a railway were made, large tracts in the interior might be turned to such good account for grazing purposes, the Colony might export cattle to England instead of importing cattle from Nova Scotia. To the valid reasons why a railway should be made is added the curious fact that this Colony is the only one of like importance wherein no railway exists.

The passage of an Act to make this railway did not end the opposition to the project. I was surprised to find men of intelligence and position disapproving of the railway and speaking with approval of the attack made by some excited women on the Surveyors. Looking over the files of the newspapers, I meet with many letters denouncing the whole matter as a dangerous innovation and treating this railway in the same terms with which railways were treated by English landowners and others when they were first introduced into England. The burden of the strain is, what was good enough for our fathers is good enough for us; that, if improvements are required they will come naturally in due course of time without any special legislation or taxation being necessary. One of the extreme opponents of the railway clenches his argument by stating that no return has yet been obtained for the money expended in making a preliminary survey. With such a man the gods would argue in vain. An explanation of much that was said and done on this subject which seemed to me incomprehensible, occurs in a number of the *Patriot and Terra Nova Herald*. There it is written that "the sole opposition to the Railroad has been created in the capital with the view of getting up a party cry. All the old shibboleths are dead. Party itself is dead or dying; and something *must* be started to give animation to the next *General Election,* and afford some chance for new aspirants to Legislative honours to become lawmakers." There is more method in the madness of such a party cry than is obvious at first sight. It is certain that the railway will not be finished for some years and, whilst under construction nothing will be so apparent as the fact of its cost. Even when finished, it will differ from nearly every railway if it should prove immediately remunerative. Thus the opponents will be able to refer to their opposition to it as to a fulfilled prophecy and may even succeed in getting people to elect them to the Legislature in order that they may cure the mischief which they have foretold. Meantime, despite covert and open opposition the railway policy of Sir William Whiteway and the Administration of which he is the head, has triumphed.

This spring the Government entered into a contract, which has been sanctioned by the Legislature for the construction of a narrow-guage line of three feet six inches from St. Johns to Hall's Bay on the north-east coast, the distance

being about 340 miles. Branches are to run to
Harbour Grace and Brigus. At a future day a
branch may be made as far as St. George's Bay on
the western shore. A New York Syndicate has
undertaken the construction and working of the
line, the line to be constructed within five years and
worked by the Company—conditionally on receiving an annual subsidy of \$180,000 for 35 years and
a grant of land, consisting of every alternate section one mile long and eight miles deep along the
line of railway. Unless the calculations made
should prove entirely misleading the Newfoundland Railway Company ought to be profitable to
its founders and beneficial to the Island in which
it will supply intercommunication by rail.

I should convey an erroneous impression if the
foregoing remarks about the railway led any
reader to suppose that I have formed a low
estimate of the Newspaper Press of Newfoundland. These journals contain foolish writing
now and then, as is the case with journals in
other places. When the writing in them is the
most extreme and severe in tone it is least easy
to imagine that the writer is perfectly in earnest
and that he is not intentionally resorting to
exaggeration. Certainly it was with a feeling of
amusement that I read in a number of *The News
Letter*, to quote but a single instance out of

many, that certain figures respecting the public debt of the Colony " show the hopeless incapacity of the present Government to rise superior to the vulgar hankering for official place and salary." The strong language which is a characteristic of these newspapers, may be in perfect accord with the taste of their readers. In consequence of this habit, the writers express a great deal more than they really mean, having no intention, when they style a man a scoundrel who is robbing the public, to convey any other idea than that they disagree with his political opinions. Sixteen newspapers are published in the Colony; my collection comprises thirteen of them. The oldest is the *Royal Gazette*, established in 1807, and having the motto "Fear God: honour the king." It contains a good selection of news as well as the official documents which are not light or very interesting reading. The *News Letter*, which was the youngest at the time I made my collection, is " devoted to the interests of the Liberal party in Newfoundland." The *Patriot and Terra Nova Herald*, which has been published for more than thirty years, prints its programme in a metrical and a prose form, the first being

> " Here shall the press the people's rights maintain,
> Unawed by influence and unbribed by gain;

> Here patriot truth her glorious precepts draw,
> Pledged to religion, liberty and Law."

The second being "Be just and fear not. Let all the ends thou aim'st at be thy God's, thy country's and truth's." The importance of developing the resources of the Island and the means for doing so are clearly apprehended and set forth by the conductors of this journal. *The Evening Telegram* is a sheet to which a writer signing himself "Au Revoir" contributes letters opposing all improvements, whether they relate to sanitary arrangements or railway communication, disparaging the politicians and professional classes and eulogizing the merchants as "the old pioneers of the country" and holding them up as the only persons whose wishes and interests ought to be considered and advanced. In *The Morning Chronicle* the policy of considering the good of the people at large is skilfully advocated and pungent letters have appeared in reply to the tirades of "Au Revoir." *The North Star* is another of the journals which treat patriotism as synonymous with the well-being of the whole community. *The Times*, which has been in existence for upwards of a generation, takes as its motto "For the Queen, the Constitution and the people." *The Newfoundlander; The Terra Nova Advocate; The Public Ledger*, and *The*

*Temperance Journal* are other journals published in St. Johns. At Harbour Grace, the next place in size to the capital, the people are enlightened and guided by the *Standard*, a large and well conducted sheet, while at two other "Outports," as all the towns save St. Johns are designated, *The Twillingate Sun* and *The Carbonear Herald* are quite as good newspapers as many published in the capital.

Though the newspaper Press does credit to the Colony, yet the credit would be greater still if a larger percentage of the people were able to profit by any printed pages. According to the census of 1876, it appears that 20,758 children did not attend school and that 18,935 did, the figures for the corresponding cases in the census of 1869 being 16,249 and 18,813. It is to be hoped that the next census will show more satisfactory results. The reports for 1879 of the Inspectors of Public Schools exhibit an attendance at school of 15,315. These Reports are from Mr. M. J. Kelly, Superintendent of the Roman Catholic Schools, of the Rev. G. S. Milligan and the Rev. William Pilot, the former being Superintendent of the Methodist, Congregational and Presbyterian, and the latter of the Church of England Schools. Mr. Kelly considers the schools under his supervision to be in a satisfactory state. Both Mr. Milligan and Mr. Pilot agree in thinking that, till attendance is made compulsory, a large number of children will grow up ignorant of the rudiments of education. Mr. Milligan holds that, while public opinion is growing in favour of educating all the children, yet that many persons will not send their children to school unless compelled by law to do so. He notes that the poorest parents are the most apathetic. He instances one case where the teacher was in fault; saying that "he was industrious, but that his education was defective." Another entry is to the effect that "at Perry's Cove, the day not being fine and the teacher aged, school was not open." He adds that this worthy old man has since retired from a position for which old age had long unfitted him. Mr Pilot is emphatic in condemning the practice of employing incompetent teachers, taking care to point out that the remedy is to pay adequate salaries in order to ensure good service. Like Mr. Milligan, he bewails the apathy and indifference of parents respecting their children's education, rightly attributing it to the fact that the parents are too ignorant themselves to appreciate the advantage of knowledge. His opinion is that "nothing short of compulsory attendance will bring about the consummation devoutly to be wished, viz., the general education of all." It is clear that the existing arrangement as to education is but provisional. Through its operation sectarian jealousy and strife have ceased. But, until all the children under twelve are obliged to attend school for a given time, it cannot be maintained that Newfoundland enjoys all the benefits which flow from a comprehensive and thorough system of national education.

Though the Island of Newfoundland is as large as England, the population numbers no more than 158,985; in Labrador which is united to it there are 2416 persons. In 1869 the total population was 146,536, so that the increase in Newfoundland and Labrador between 1869 and 1876 was 14,836. Considering the nature and extent of the Island, the number of persons inhabiting it is absurdly small. The mass of the people find it hard to earn daily bread. Upwards of $100,000 are expended annually in relieving the poor. The misfortune of the people consists in the fishery being their only means of livelihood and that they do not seem disposed to embrace any others. Indeed they look with suspicion upon any harvest except that of the sea. They have a saying that an acre of the sea is worth a thousand acres of land.

It has been proved that the Island abounds in excellent timber, that there is grazing-ground sufficient for rearing thousands of cattle, that there is land enough to grow all the grain required for home consumption and leave a large surplus for export. I have examined the Customs Returns for 1879 and I observe that the following articles, all of which might be produced in the Island, were imported to the extent specified: Flour 303,483 barrels; oatmeal 1884 barrels; meat and poultry to the value of $28,479; peas 4445 barrels; salt 42,943 tons; timber 341 tons; potatoes 109,380 bushels; other vegetables 24,428 bushels; hay and straw 596 tons; shingles 42,943 tons. These are some of the articles which ought to be produced in the Island and which might be exported in place of being imported. Among the curiosities of those returns is an entry among the exports of 27 gallons of Spanish red wine having been sent to Spain. This is a new version of sending coal to Newcastle.

If the Reformation had taken place at an earlier day and been universal, or had not the Church of Rome made a fish diet obligatory on many days in the year, it is doubtful whether the Newfoundland fisheries or those of the Cornish fisheries either, would have attained their present value. Next to the United Kingdom, the country to which Newfoundland exports the most is Brazil.

I subjoin the list which I have arranged in accordance with the amounts exported to each:—

| | |
|---|---:|
| The United Kingdom | $2,067,636 |
| Brazil | 1,383,819 |
| Portugal | 713,571 |
| Spain | 584,427 |
| The Dominion of Canada | 316,630 |
| United States of America | 268,018 |
| British West Indies | 231,848 |
| Italy | 131,493 |
| Gibraltar | 84,840 |
| Hamburg | 49,139 |
| French West Indies | 40,469 |
| Sicily | 12,012 |
| Sainte Pierre | 8,903 |
| Mauritius | 8,671 |
| Jersey | 8,199 |
| Madeira | 7,101 |
| France | 2,148 |

By arranging the imports in the order of values, it will be seen that several countries, to which the exports are the largest, send the smallest proportion of goods in return.

| | |
|---|---:|
| The Dominion of Canada | $2,258,671 |
| The United Kingdom | 2,180,703 |
| United States of America | 2,140,345 |
| British West Indies | 329,220 |
| Spain | 172,704 |
| French West Indies | 101,738 |
| Portugal | 20,980 |
| Jersey | 19,374 |
| Sicily | 11,417 |
| Hamburg | 4,502 |
| France | 605 |

Four places, Brazil, Gibraltar, Madeira, Mauritius, to which the exports amount to $1,484,440 send nothing back to Newfoundland. The result is that the value of the total exports is $5,918,924, while that of the imports is $7,261,002.

Among the exports are 28,405 tons of copper ore valued at $511,290 and $1112\frac{1}{2}$ tons of regulus valued at $44,500. These are the results of mining at Betts Cove and Little Bay carried on by a company formed by Mr. Ellershausen of Nova Scotia. In the brief space of five years Newfoundland has risen to the sixth place among the copper-producing regions of the globe. Other minerals have been discovered in sufficient quantities to justify their extraction; these include gold and silver, nickel, lead and iron. Coal-beds of vast extent, though known to exist, have not yet been worked. It seems probable, however, that when the mineral deposits on the Island are systematically explored and made available it may become as famous and envied for its mines as for its fisheries. At present the merchants, who are the capitalists of Newfoundland, give their attention to the fisheries and neglect alike its mineral and agricultural resources.

A company has been formed for prosecuting copper-mining on an extensive scale. It is styled the Newfoundland Consolidated Copper Mining Company and its originators are citizens of the United States, the head office being in New York.

Mr. Ellershausen transferred to this company the properties over which he had control. Other properties have been acquired and the undertaking, as a whole, is gigantic. The capital is in keeping, being three million dollars. Should this company be as successful as its sanguine promoters anticipate, a great impetus will be given to mining in Newfoundland.

As the Island is peopled and if a railway be constructed to St. George's Bay, a question of international relations will have to be finally determined. Between Newfoundland and the United States frequent disputes have arisen concerning the fisheries, but these are even less complicated and more easily settled than the chronic misunderstanding with France on the same subject.

The misunderstanding known as the Fortune Bay outrage has been dispelled by Great Britain paying 15,000*l.* in full of all demands for compensation from the New England fishermen who were maltreated by the Newfoundlanders. Other differences of opinion as to the true interpretation of clauses in the Treaty of Washington may yet be harmonized by diplomacy. That treaty is as noteworthy as other similar documents for the vagueness of its terms. This appears to be the great object of diplomatists. Just as plumbers seem to take care to leave some damaged pipes when they are called in to put the water supply to a house in good order and do so with the hope of being soon summoned to repair the mischief they have wrought, so diplomatists continue to leave treaties in such a condition that controversy arises as to their precise purport and fresh negotiations have to be undertaken with a view to make their terms intelligible and satisfactory to the persons affected. The treaty of Utrecht, which defines the rights of the French at the coast of Newfoundland, might be regarded as an exception to the rule, as it is as clear as any instrument of the kind. Yet it has been held by the French to confer rights which do not seem to have occurred to its framers.

By that treaty the French enjoy the right, confirmed by subsequent treaties, of fishing off the west coast of Newfoundland and of drying fish on the shore, concurrently with the subjects of the British Sovereign. This has been interpreted by French diplomatists to mean an exclusive right both to the fishery and to the occupation of the western shore. As Lord Palmerston observed, in a masterly despatch on the subject to Count Sebastiani in 1838, a concurrent right of enjoyment cannot possibly mean an exclusive right to a particular privilege; he added, "the claim put forward on the part of France is founded simply upon inference, and upon an assumed interpretation of words." Yet the French have protested against mining operations on the plea that the land must be reserved for their exclusive use. The district about which this dispute exists is the favourite resort of persons who have imperative reasons for disliking the police and who like this region because policemen are unknown in it. The points at issue between France and this country concerning Newfoundland become more embarrassing as time passes away. In such a case as this, delay is unquestionably dangerous. The sooner a clear and definite understanding is arrived at the better for all parties. By a system of bounties the French have given their fishermen a practical monopoly of fishing on the Banks of Newfoundland; not a single British vessel being able to compete with them. This they are free to do, but no valid authority has yet been shown by them for excluding British subjects from British soil. When the matter is again dealt with, it would be wise if the statesmen of Newfoundland were represented on any commission which might be empowered to act; the question immediately concerns them and it is one with which they are intimately acquainted.

I have shown how much there is in Newfoundland to attract and enrich the woodman, the farmer and the miner, in addition to the original attraction which has made it the great home of fishermen. It may yet be numbered among the spots to which invalids hasten in order to regain health by drinking mineral water. There are many mineral springs in the Island which only require puffing to be popular. A chalybeate spring at Logie Bay, near St. Johns, resembles the spring at Bath which used to be most in request when that place was the fashionable resort for all sorts and conditions of invalids. The seeker after sport will there find as good opportunities of gratifying his taste as he can in the hunting-grounds of the Far West. The rivers abound in salmon, the inland lakes teem with trout; cariboo are still numerous and bears are often met with. Feathered game are plentiful. Anyone who desires to combine sport with profit can hunt wolves. Under an Act of the Legislature a reward of $12 is paid for the head of every wolf killed. Mosquitoes and other insects are even greater plagues than wolves, causing more annoyance and being less easily exterminated. On the other hand, the Island enjoys immunity from frogs, toads, lizards and all venomous reptiles. It has long been noted for its dogs. In the earlier days of its history there is frequent mention of wild cats and hawks being brought from Newfoundland to England. Later the Newfoundland dog grew into repute and was deservedly prized. When the Prince of Wales visited the Island in 1861 a splendid dog of pure breed was presented to him which he appropriately named Cabot. The Islanders cannot make many such gifts now. They have innumerable dogs, but most of them are mongrels which no rational person would accept as a gift.

The resources of "England's Oldest Colony" are greater; its soil and climate are far better; its natural attractions are more varied, than is commonly supposed. Among these I do not number the public debt of $1,240,990, bearing interest at the moderate rate of 4 per cent. Yet no independent state or self-governing colony has a debt which has been incurred for more useful objects and which imposes so light and temporary a burden upon the community. The bonds, which were issued at par, are at a premium. In the statement of accounts for last year, the Auditor remarks that the public debt of the Colony is "held solely by the people of Newfoundland." The Islanders ought to be prouder of this fact than of the many advantages which Nature has placed within their reach.

# CHAPTER II.

### THE LAND OF THE "BLUE NOSES."

The Royal Province of Nova Scotia, as its inhabitants proudly style it, is familiar to readers of "Sam Slick" as the home of "the Blue Noses." The late Mr. Justice Haliburton, the author of "Sam Slick," was a member of the House of Assembly of Nova Scotia when a young man, and he died, at an advanced age, a member of the Parliament of the United Kingdom. He did not object to the nickname which the Yankees had given to his fellow-countrymen; on the contrary he thought it an honour to be "a Blue Nose." One of the most accomplished and estimable of New England poets has embalmed in harmonious verse a sad and romantic episode in Nova Scotia's early history. Indeed, the legendary history of this Province has received a circulation through Mr. Longfellow's "Evangeline" far wider than that of its authentic and more prosaic records.

Sir William Alexander, the founder of Nova Scotia, was accounted a good poet in his day. His verses pleased James the First, who called him "my philosophical poet." He was a consummate courtier; he excelled in the art of persuading Princes to confer upon him substantial tokens of their favour. The Province of Nova Scotia was a gift to him from James the First. His son Charles made the further grant of the power to create Baronets to the number of 150 as a means of promoting the settlement of the Province. Each Baronet was to acquire 6000 acres of land in return for a payment of 150*l*. A special privilege, which they much valued and which some of their contemporaries deservedly ridiculed, was to wear a yellow ribbon round their necks from which hung the badge of their order. This excited the jealously of the Irish and English Baronets who petitioned that they, too, might display a similar token of their rank. Sir William Alexander did not find his Province or his order of Baronets so remunerative as the permission to coin base money. With the wealth thus acquired he built himself a fine house at Stirling. Sir William's wealth would have been greater still if the people of Scotland would have consented to adopt in their churches the Metrical version of the Psalms made by James the First and revised by him. Charles the First ordered that the version should be used, but the people objecting to it as decidedly as they did to Laud's Prayer Book, the monopoly of printing that version for thirty-one years, conferred upon Sir William Alexander, did not profit the "philosophical poet." He died bearing the title of Earl of Stirling without having effected anything else for Nova Scotia than to give it a name. Through great tribulation that Province has slowly attained its present condition as the chief among the Maritime Provinces of the Dominion of Canada.

When the Confederation of Canada was achieved in 1867, a strong protest was made by Nova Scotians against becoming members of the Dominion. The Hon. Joseph Howe, the soul and leader of the malcontents visited England and enlisted Mr. Bright's powerful advocacy in appealing to Parliament to detach Nova Scotia from the new Confederation. The attempt failed ; Mr. Howe was pacified, after what were called "better terms" had been offered to the Province and then he accepted office in the Government of the Dominion. The controversy as to the advantage of Confederation has not yet lost all bitterness, or ceased to excite and divide the people of this Province. Superadded to it is the question of that "National Policy" which Sir John Macdonald devised and to which the Dominion Parliament has given effect at the instance of his Administration. "National Policy" is the old-fashioned "Protection to native industry" under a new form and with a new name. Some Nova Scotians declare that the evils of Confederation have been intensified by the effects of protection. Others are of opinion that the severe depression felt in business circles during the last few years is due to general causes affecting the entire commercial world. For six or seven years after Confederation, the Province enjoyed extraordinary prosperity. Large sums were then expended in constructing railways, cutting canals, erecting public buildings throughout the Dominion, and this Province shared in the business activity which ensued when so much borrowed capital was put into circulation. Merchants and others lived up to their means; sometimes they lived beyond them in the belief that the gains of the future would more than meet any liability they might incur, and thus, when the day of reckoning suddenly and unexpectedly arrived, the reaction was the more disastrous because the expansion had been so extreme. It is a gross blunder to blame Confederation for this. Nor would it be discreet to pronounce that the new panacea for making everybody rich and contented has utterly failed.

A protective policy ought to succeed for a time, and it will continue popular so long as the people at large are satisfied to pay the price. An individual who is rich enough can have any luxury which money will buy. Protection is a luxury which only a very wealthy or a very self-denying nation can afford to pay for. As yet the influence of the "National" or protective policy of Canada has had so slight an effect in this Province that although the Nova Scotians rail against it, they are influenced by their fears rather than by their actual experience.

The most doleful and dispiriting account which I received as to the position and prospects of Nova Scotia was supplied by a Virginian gentleman, who played a leading part in the tragedy of secession and who has made his home in Halifax. His heart is in his native State but his money is invested in the capital of Nova Scotia. He assured me that the Nova Scotians had ceased to be loyal to the British Empire and would have no objection to become citizens of the North American Republic. I failed to ascertain any ground for this conclusion; but I heard that, house property having fallen in value, this gentleman's invested capital has been reduced for the moment. Should land and houses rise in price he may change his views. Despite his dissatisfaction with the policy of the Government under which he had voluntarily chosen to live, he had no fault to find with the Province as a place of abode; on the contrary, he praised both the soil and climate in strong terms. Natives of the country deplored the emigration from it of young men to the United States. Communication between Halifax and Boston in Massachusetts is frequent and the journey can be made for a small outlay. The temptation is extreme for young Nova Scotians, who are dissatisfied with their home prospects, to proceed to New England in order to begin life there under conditions which they consider more favourable. They are influenced by the feeling which causes the country bumpkin to quit his quiet English village and hasten to London where he hopes to find the streets paved with gold. Many Nova Scotians learn by sad experience that, if they are better paid abroad, they must work harder and expend more than at home, and the numbers of the disenchanted and disappointed who return are said to balance the numbers who depart elate and over sanguine.

Intelligent Nova Scotians whose opinions on other subjects would have commanded my respect, spoke concerning the Canadian Pacific Railway with a recklessness which astonished me. They laboured under the delusion that the construction of the Railway would either ruin the Dominion or else that the operation of the railway would benefit the Western Provinces exclusively. If a citizen of New York were to use similar language in reference to the Union Pacific Railway, his hearers would naturally conclude that he had lost his wits. The truth is that Halifax will profit by a railway through Canada from the Atlantic to the Pacific just as New York city has profited by the railway between that city and San Francisco.

The evidence which I have collected leads me to the conclusion that the Nova Scotians are too ready to grumble and are deficient in a patriotic faith in the resources of Canada and in the capacity of her sons to develope them. In Halifax there are many men who are irreverently but not inaptly termed " old fossils." They have made enough money upon which to live in comfort. They have invested it in non-speculative securities yielding them a moderate return. They have adequate capital wherewith to embark in any enterprise, but they lack the requisite courage for supporting novel undertakings with their money, even though the chance of doubling their capital and income by so doing may not be slight. These men are foremost in complaining of capital and energy being lacking to develope Nova Scotia's resources. It has been proved to demonstration that the gold fields are as rich and as safe investments as the coal pits from which adventurous native and English capitalists have derived large profits. The Nova Scotian capitalist hesitates to take shares in a gold-mine. When a gold-mine of undoubted richness is discovered and tested, it usually passes into the hands of a shrewd and enterprising United States capitalist, and when the Nova Scotians see him becoming rich by his venture they blame Confederation or the Government for marring the prosperity of their Province. After the discovery of gold in 1861 at Tangier River, forty miles to the east of Halifax, there was an outburst of foolish speculation. When over-cautious men lose their heads, they are frequently guilty of inconceivable follies. Experience then taught the lesson that a gold-mine may absorb more of the precious metal than it can ever yield, and that it is necessary to exercise judgment in choosing a mine and skill in working it. The Nova Scotians seem disposed to act like a boy who, having burned his fingers, refuses ever after to warm his hands at the fire. Instead of profiting, in a rational way, by what has occurred, their prevailing feeling now is to eschew mining altogether and let strangers step in and carry off the golden prizes.

From the year that the extraction of gold began down to the present time, the total yield has been

397,372 ounces. Last year 14,000 ounces were returned. The average earning of each miner has exceeded $600 annually; the earning last year exceeded $700. These figures contrast most favourably with returns from other regions of this Continent where gold-mining is a remunerative industry. Yet the room for improvement here is very great. The waste in extracting gold is enormous. It is indisputable that a yield of five pennyweights per ton is ample for paying the miner who uses the most improved machinery and follows the most modern processes. Gold-mines in Brazil and Australia, where the return is at that rate, pay large profits, yet in Nova Scotia the complaint is that no profit can be obtained unless the quartz yield ten pennyweights per ton, seven being a common yield and seven being found inadequate for profitable working.

Mr. Selwyn, the Director of the Geological Survey of Canada who, for sixteen years before filling that office, filled an analogous one in Victoria, has shown how close are many of the geological resemblances between the Provinces of Victoria and Nova Scotia. He also shows how wasteful the system of mining is in the latter Province, many mines there wasting as much as would suffice to return dividends of 10 per cent. in Victoria, and the machinery in the Australian mines doing nearly double as much work as that employed in the Nova Scotian. It is clear that skill and proper machinery are lacking. Were the Nova Scotian gold-mines properly developed they would take rank among the most remunerative, favourite and stable investments of the Province. The gold-bearing region of Nova Scotia extends over 3000 square miles.

Coal and Iron are two products of which Nova Scotia possesses an abundance. The capital invested in coal winning is estimated at $12,000,000; the number of pits worked is twenty-five. Pictou, which is the principal town in the coal district, is next in importance to Halifax. It is picturesquely situated on a point jutting into a land-locked harbour wherein hundreds of vessels can be conveniently moored. The passage from Northumberland Straits into the harbour is only 200 yards across at the entrance. On either side the eye rests upon a stretch of fine land dotted with trees and divided into farms. The town of Pictou was founded in 1767 by some emigrants from Philadelphia. Five years afterwards thirty families arrived from the Scottish Highlands with the object of establishing a settlement, but, being unable to agree with the first comers as to the right of ownership in the land, they went elsewhere. Other families from Scotland arrived here at a later day, and the majority of the people still bear Scottish names and speak with the accent of their forefathers. The demand for Nova Scotian coal is greater now than in former years. The trade with the United States, which was almost extinct for a time, has revived again. I saw three United States vessels taking in cargoes, a sight which, as I was informed, was both unusual and welcome. When the Reciprocity Treaty was in force, Nova Scotian coal was chiefly exported to the United States; since the imposition of a heavy import duty, that market has ceased to be the principal one. The coal-owners complain that the present Canadian tariff does not give them that monopoly of supplying the Western Provinces of the Dominion which they expected to have under the "National policy." The citizens of Ontario still buy coal imported from the United States, while the citizens of New England still buy coal imported from Nova Scotia. A protective tariff cannot always subserve the design of its framers either by diverting all trade into a particular channel or in diffusing universal happiness.

A short ride from South Pictou brings the traveller to New Glasgow, which resembles the ancient and flourishing city on the banks of the Clyde in being over-hung with smoke. Not far distant are the Albion pits, from which large quantities of coal have been taken for half a century, and which are expected to continue productive for many years to come. The seam there is thirty feet thick. At New Glasgow there are iron foundries, tanneries, a pottery and ship-building yards. The largest Nova Scotian ships have been built here. This industry was not brisk at the time of my visit; I saw only one ship on the stocks. The demand for wooden vessels is falling off and, if the ship-builders here would regain their supremacy, they must build iron ships. They have so many facilities for so doing that, by taking due advantage of them, the iron vessels of Glasgow in Nova Scotia might be in as great request as those of Glasgow in Old Scotland. The Island of Cape Breton, another part of this Province wherein coal abounds, is about a mile from the mainland, being separated from it by the Gut of Canso. The scenery on this island, which attracts tourists quite as much as the coal-fields attract capitalists, is on a very grand scale. Readers of Horace Walpole's writings will remember an amusing reference to this Island. Walpole asserts that the Duke of Newcastle, the Prime Minister at the time, having learnt to his surprise that Cape Breton was an Island, he could not rest till he had communicated the extraordinary fact to every member of the Cabinet.

From Cape Breton at the north to Yarmouth at the south, this Province covers an area of nearly 22,000 square miles, out of which 3000 square miles are covered with lakes. It has a coast-line of 1200 miles and a large number of excellent harbours. Within the limits of the Province, which is about 300 miles long by from 100 to 50 in breadth, there are great varieties of soil and climate; the temperature is 8° higher in the western than in the eastern Counties. It has plenty of shaggy wood, but no mountains like those in Old Scotia. The height of the hills does not exceed 1000 feet. The richest and most picturesque part of the Province is the broad valley between Windsor and Annapolis, where the Acadians passed an existence which resembles the visions of the golden age.

The historian of Nova Scotia, depicting their state in 1755, tells how these Acadians, to the number of 18,000 tilled the fields, reaped crops, and reared cattle and poultry in this happy valley. Their ordinary drink was beer or cyder. They clad themselves in garments spun from the flax which they cultivated or from the fleece of their sheep. They rarely went to law, accepting the decision of the elders in cases of dispute.

There was no permanent destitution among them, the unfortunate being succoured by those richer in the world's goods. They lived as a large and happy family; early marriages were the rule and the vices of great cities were unknown. The picture of these people before their expulsion makes their fate seem the more pitiful; but it may be that the picture is too highly coloured and that the Annapolis Valley has never been the scene of an earthly paradise. It is certainly a pleasant and fruitful land where the inhabitants have every reason to enjoy life. The soil is very fertile and admirably adapted for the growth of fruit trees. Indeed, the apples grown in the Annapolis Valley are very fine and are highly prized by good judges. When the apple trees are in blossom the prospect resembles that between Heidelberg and Frankfort in the spring time when the cherry trees are in blossom. It is a peculiarity of this Province to offer great variety of scenery and of means of livelihood. The farmer, gardener, miner and fisherman can all find profitable employment. The fisheries are very valuable; the fish caught comprise cod, mackerel, shad, hake, herring and salmon; the annual return from the fisheries is not much under a million sterling. Twenty thousand men are occupied in fishing. The land is specially well suited for the culture of such vegetables as potatoes and turnips, and of such grains as wheat, barley, oats, rye, buckwheat and maize. The number of acres of good land is estimated at 10,000,000. Of these less than 2,000,000 are under cultivation. This large, fertile and salubrious Province, wherein there is ample scope for millions of people, has less than 400,000 inhabitants.

Halifax is the capital of Nova Scotia. It has many natural advantages among which beauty of situation is the most striking and that of possessing the finest harbour on the coast is the most useful. It was founded on the 25th July 1749. Not till the close of the American revolutionary war did it secure a large accession of citizens. Then, however, it became a refuge for the United Empire Loyalists who abandoned or were expelled from their homes in the United States. These men displayed great vigour and fortitude in promoting the interests of this Province. They gave an impetus to the capital which it has not quite lost or which, if lost is owing to the accident of their descendants not inheriting all their virtues and all their talents. My opinion is that the sluggishness of the generation now passing away will give place to greater energy in the generation which is growing up and that the new comers will revive the best traditions of Nova Scotia by working as strenuously to make it an ornament to the Dominion as their forefathers did to render it a model Province.

The capital of Nova Scotia is the only place in the Dominion where a British garrison is maintained. It is the only city on the North American Continent where a Government dockyard is kept up by the United Kingdom. The dockyard covers fourteen acres. Men-of-war are always to be seen in the harbour, soldiers of all arms are to be seen in the streets and these things give liveliness to the scene. The citizens have sometimes reason to regret that soldiers are stationed here. When a discontented private determines to do the utmost mischief with the least suffering to himself, he smashes the costly plate-glass windows in the principal shops. I once passed along a street where this wanton destruction of property was perpetrated so quickly that no one could prevent it. The shopkeeper would get no compensation if the glass were uninsured. The soldier would probably be imprisoned for a time and then dismissed the service. However unwelcome the presence of the troops may sometimes be, I am sure that a proposal to withdraw them altogether would not please everybody. As a garrison town Halifax has many charms for strangers, especially for citizens of the United States. Of late years many of these citizens spend the summer months here, the climate at that season being excellent and the sea-bathing being all that can be desired. If a large and well-appointed hotel were built at or near to the lovely North West Arm, which is the rural part of Halifax and where many charming villas are built, the influx of strangers would be greater than ever. The Halifax Hotel, though good and comfortable, does not meet the requirements of exacting visitors from the United States. Although the hotels are disappointing, no fault can be found with the Halifax Club. It is admirably managed. The building is commodious and the stranger who, like myself, is honoured by being temporarily allowed to use it, finds his stay in Halifax rendered far more agreeable, while his regret at leaving it is far more keen. What Marryat wrote in *Peter Simple* is still true : " All sailors agree in asserting that Halifax is one of the most delightful ports in which a ship can anchor. Everybody is hospitable, cheerful, and willing to amuse and be amused."

The Capital of Nova Scotia is not only a splendid port for commerce, but it is also one of the strongest fortified places in the world. The Duke of Kent, the father of the Queen, planned the Citadel and laid its foundations. There is a belief that the ground upon which the Citadel stands is rich in gold quartz. If this be well founded, then the defenders of the Citadel have a twofold treasure to guard. The fortifications on the islands in the Bay are so well planned and executed that a hostile attack upon the city may be regarded with equanimity, because it can be repelled with certainty. Through the courtesy of Colonel Drayson, an officer of large experience and multifarious accomplishments who was in command of the artillery at the time of my visit, I visited the fortifications and was permitted to inspect them in detail. Nothing that the science of war could suggest in the way of defence has been overlooked in their arrangement or neglected in their supervision. Everything is in perfect order and available at any moment. Should an enemy attack them, he will have a painfully warm reception and he will egregiously err if he should count upon finding the defenders napping. Visitors from the United States are shown whatever they want to see and they leave the place with the conviction that, if the hotels are not perfect, the fortifications are of the first class.

The Provincial Legislature meets in Halifax. Close to the building where the Legislators

assemble is a large building containing the
Government offices, the Post office, the City
Library and the Provincial Museum, the latter
being rich in the antiquities, Indian relics and
mineral products of the Province. I ought not
to omit to mention with well-deserved praise the
public garden, which is not only extensive and
stocked with curious plants, but which is kept
with as much care as it is laid out with taste. Nor
should I conclude without writing a few sentences
in eulogy of the present Lieutenant-Governor, Mr.
Archibald, who occupies an official residence
which has a gloomy look, but which is a commodious and most agreeable house to live in.
Mr. Archibald is a Nova Scotian and his ambition
is centred in advancing the interest of his native
Province. He has had long and varied experience of public life and he has played his part
in it most admirably. He filled the office of
Lieutenant-Governor of Manitoba at a crisis in
the history of that far western member of the
Dominion, and he there displayed great administrative ability, solving the difficult problem of
reconciling the Indians to their new Canadian
rulers and concluding treaties with them which
have proved as just to them as they have been
serviceable to Canada. If his fellow-countrymen
in Nova Scotia were imbued with his patriotic

spirit and were endowed with his capacity for dealing with problems in public affairs, the progress of their fine Province would be even more rapid and gratifying in the future than it has been in the past. That the " Royal Province " has a great future I firmly believe. That "the Blue Noses" have great opportunities as well as honourable traditions is quite certain. Their land offers many inducements to the capitalist and it is a tempting home for the emigrant. The capitalist, the mining engineer, the agriculturist, the sportsman and the emigrant can all find within the ample and untenanted limits of Nova Scotia, an incomparable field wherein to realize the fondest desires of their hearts.

# CHAPTER III.

### THE PROVINCE OF NEW BRUNSWICK.

WHEN St. John, the chief city of New Brunswick, was almost entirely destroyed by fire on the 20th of June, 1877, the loss sustained was greater proportionately than that caused by the great fire at Chicago six years previously. About 13,000 New Brunswickers were then rendered homeless; 1612 houses, covering an area of 200 acres, were destroyed in the brief space of nine hours; the loss of property was estimated at $27,000,000. English philanthropists showed their usual and laudable alacrity in aiding the sufferers. Some of them also displayed discreditable ignorance about the situation of St. John and the nationality of its inhabitants. I remember an appeal earnestly made by one of them to the effect that the sad occasion was an admirable opportunity, not only for succouring the needy, but also for manifesting brotherly love and charity towards the citizens of the United States. Unfortunately, this is no isolated example of geographical ignorance. Indeed, when Cobden expressed his opinion that young Englishmen should be instructed in the history of Chicago, he might have added that they would be all the better for obtaining precise knowledge of the history and geography of Canada. This knowledge would prove quite as useful to them as that minute and exclusive acquaintance with Grecian history and literature which he assumed them to possess and which, as an intellectual possession, he may have undervalued.

It is true that the people of New Brunswick are closely allied in race to their neighbours across the border. Many of the oldest and most respected New Brunswick families are descended from the Loyalists who were driven from the United States because they pertinaciously avowed their predilection for an ideal British Empire of which the North American Continent should form a part. No Province of the Dominion of Canada is less Yankee in sentiment than New Brunswick which is conterminous on the south-west with the State of Maine. Its inhabitants do not seem to have forgotten how the State of Maine was aggrandized at the expense of their Province in 1842, owing to what they believe to have been the sharp practice of Daniel Webster, then Secretary of State in Mr. Tyler's Administration.

The Puritans of Massachusetts played a curious part in the early history of what is now New Brunswick but was then called Acadia. John Winthrop, then Governor of Massachusetts, assented to a request that New England ships and men should be employed in helping Latour, who held the fort which stood on the site of the principal city in the Province and who refused to surrender it, and resign his commission of Lieutenant-General to D'Aulnay whom the King of France had sent to supersede him. The assistance rendered by the New Englanders proving effectual, D'Aulnay had to retire discomfited. This happened in 1643. Two years afterwards D'Aulnay renewed the attack during Latour's absence. The wife of Latour then displayed the heroic qualities which the Countess of Derby afterwards did during the war between the English Parliament and Charles the First. Again, D'Aulnay was repulsed. A third time he made the attempt and, on this occasion, he succeeded through bribery in getting a footing in the fort though vigorously opposed by Madame Latour at the head of fifty brave men. His revenge consisted in hanging the whole garrison before the eyes of the woman who had manifested so much fortitude and bravery. The spectacle was more terrible to her than an assault of armed men; she died of grief soon after.

When D'Aulnay felt himself strong enough to assert his rights, he accused the Government of Massachusetts with a breach of neutrality and demanded compensation. The latter replied that they had not directly interfered in the quarrel, having merely permitted Latour to hire ships and enlist men. The damages demanded were 8000*l.*, yet the Commissioner who urged the claims of D'Aulnay said that if the Government acknowledged their guilt in the matter the damages might be reduced to a nominal amount. Ultimately the blame was transferred to Captain Hawkins and the volunteers who had taken part with Latour, and the Government consented "to send a small present to D'Aulnay in satisfaction of what Captain Hawkins and the others had done." Governor Winthrop in describing the transaction, enables us to understand that the "smartness" which is supposed to be a modern characteristic of New England was possessed and exercised by the early Puritans. The small present sent to D'Aulnay was "a very fair new sedan" which had been taken in the West Indies and presented to the Governor, which was "worth forty or fifty pounds where it was made, but of no use to us."¹

In 1650, Latour returned. D'Aulnay had died in the interval, leaving a widow who surrendered the fort to Latour and, three years afterwards, became his wife. Thus Latour not only regained possession of the fort but he became the husband of his rival's wife and lord of all his lands. This settlement occurred in 1653; in the following year it was abruptly terminated by Oliver Cromwell who sent a naval expedition against him with the result that he was ousted from office and Acadia was annexed to England. It was ceded to France again a few years later and it was re-acquired by England in 1745; a few years after this an English garrison under the command of Colonel Moncton was established in the fort which, during a century, had been the subject of strife. A few settlers came hither from England in 1764; but the first settlement on a large scale and permanent basis was made by 5000 United Empire Loyalists who left the United States in 1783 and, on the 18th of May in that year, founded the city of St. John. Several years later there was an influx of settlers from Ireland who have found their removal to the new country from the old one to be highly advan-

[1] John Winthrop's "New England," vol. ii. p. 274.

tageous. The least successful tillers of the soil appear to be the descendants of the Acadians who escaped expulsion from the country. Their farming is both slovenly and wasteful, consisting in exhausting a piece of land and then applying to the Government for a new piece whereon to recommence the same process.

Many small colonies have settled in New Brunswick and have prospered exceedingly. A small colony numbering 182 went thither from the North of England in 1837. The colonists had to fell trees before they could cultivate the land. According to a return compiled in the sixth year of their sojourn, the result of their labour was that they had taken from land originally covered with trees, 260 tons of hay and straw, and 1500 bushels of grain, potatoes and turnips. They appended to the return the following remarks: "The climate of New Brunswick agrees well with the constitution of Englishmen; the air is salubrious, and the water as pure and wholesome as any in the world. During the six years of our location there have occurred but two deaths, while there have been thirty-nine births without the presence of medical aid. Six years' experience have convinced us that notwithstanding the privations to which new settlers are exposed, diligence and perseverance must ensure success." In 1842, an attempt was made to found a small colony of Irish people where teetotal principles would be rigorously practised. The experiment was successful beyond expectation. The colony, including women and children, numbered 101. Thirty male members of it are credited at the end of the first year with having gathered from a spot, which had been a dense forest till they cleared it, 7276 bushels of grain, potatoes and turnips. Their labour had been rewarded with a total return, in crops and permanent improvements, to the value of 2000*l*.

Quite as interesting and significant as any of the foregoing examples is that of the Danish colony established within the last ten years about eight miles from Grand Falls in the western part of the Province. This place, formerly called Hellerup, is now known as New Denmark. There it was that, in the year 1872, thirty-six Danes began to cut down the primeval forest. The toil was harder than they had counted upon, while the difficulties against which they contended seemed so great as to dishearten them. But they persevered and they have now no reason to complain. Where trees covered the ground a few years ago, is now a tract of cleared land extending over 3000 acres and yielding large crops. The colony has grown from 36 to 500 persons and it is being recruited by frequent arrivals; as many as 120 immigrants arrived there from Denmark in 1879. The extent of the settlement is such that there are thirty-six miles of road running through it. The people are frugal and industrious, and are growing rich, because they have an annual surplus in excess of their own requirements. A curious circumstance is that, whereas the Danes who arrived here were Lutherans, they adopted the service of the Church of England in the church which they built for themselves.

All the facts which I have gleaned from official papers as to the prosperity of the New Brunswick farmers were verified in conversation with those whom I questioned as to their condition. They have many advantages over farmers in the Far West. The land yields as good a return, while the price obtained for the produce is higher owing to the proximity of a market. They have not to pay so much for what they buy, as the farmers must do who are far removed from the sea-board, while they receive more for what they have to sell than the farmers can do whose crops have to be carried to market hundreds of miles by rail. The area of the Province is 27,332 square miles, being greater than that of the Kingdoms of Belgium and Holland combined. Thirteen million of acres are available for cultivation. It is estimated that the land can support a population numbering four millions and a half. The actual population does not much exceed three hundred thousand!

The St. John River is the most notable fact in the Province of New Brunswick. It is a noble stream, affording, with its tributaries, 1300 miles of navigable waters, draining a region covering 17,000,000 acres, thereof 9,000,000 are within the Province, 2,000,000 in the Province of Quebec, and 6,000,000 in the State of Maine. The valley through which it flows is very beautiful, the scenery being quite as attractive as at the most lovely parts of the Hudson. The Indians gave it the name "Looshtook" because they were struck with its length, the word meaning "Long River." It winds through the Province for a distance of 250 miles; as the Province is 190 miles long by 140 broad, it is obvious that the St. John River is a meandering stream. At the upper part of the stream are Grand Falls where the water descends 70 feet perpendicularly. Where it enters the harbour at the city of St. John another fall of a singular kind attracts the notice of strangers. When the tide is out and the water low, the water descends 17 feet. At high water, on the contrary, the fall, if I may thus phrase it, is in the opposite direction, the tide rising so high as to cause rapids up stream. I passed over the spot in a steamer during the twenty minutes this can be done when the tide is at its height, and I could scarcely realize that the spot was the same as that at which I had seen the river dashing down the rocks in a sheet of foam.

For some distance above the city of St. John the river is very wide and is studded with wooded islands. The view on either side is varied and most attractive over the whole eighty-six miles which intervene between that city and Fredericton, the Capital of the Province. The Lieutenant-Governor occupies an official residence at Fredericton which is imposing in appearance but which has a serious defect, judging from the statement which Dr. Botsford, a physician of St. John, made in a paper read before the Convention at Ottawa of the Canada Medical Association. Dr. Botsford said that Government House, which cost $100,000 to erect and from $5000 to $8000 annually to maintain, was so unhealthy that the persons who lived there did so at their peril. The sudden death of the late Lieutenant-Governor and the ill-health of the present one were attributable, in his opinion, to the sewage gas which pervades the edifice. It is clear, then, that the Governor of this Province runs quite as much risk as the leader of a forlorn hope. Let me hope, however, that Government House will be converted into a

place, in which to enjoy life, from one in which to
risk and lose it. A house of meeting for the
Provincial Legislature is the most recent public
building in Fredericton; it has been erected to
replace the one destroyed by fire. The new
House of Assembly is a substantial stone structure. The Episcopal Cathedral is the building
most conspicuous and best worthy of a visit.
This Cathedral vies with that of Montreal as a
fine example of Canadian ecclesiastical architecture. The loyal citizens take pleasure in informing a stranger that the altar-cloth is the one
used at the coronation of William the Fourth.
The Methodists have built a church with a spire
still higher than that of the Cathedral and having
a hand with an outstretched finger at the summit.
Much of this structure is of wood, and it does not
resist the action of the weather like the stone of
which the Cathedral is built; thus, while the
Methodists are entitled to boast of having the
higher spire, they have also the obligation of
paying largely to keep it in repair. The University of New Brunswick, founded in 1800, is at
Fredericton. An annual scholarship of $60 is
awarded to one boy from each county in the Province as well as free tuition, and fifty-six scholarships, entitling the holder to free tuition, are
appropriated for competition to any youth in the

cities and counties. The Methodists founded a College at Sackville in 1862 which is open to students of either sex, and the Roman Catholics maintain St. Joseph's College at Memramcook.

The Post office, and other public buildings in Fredericton are of red brick; several stores and warehouses are built of the same material; they have all a solid appearance and they belong to men who are enterprising and opulent. Trees line the streets and surround many of the buildings. Gardens are attached to most of the houses and the combination of foliage and flowers on every hand, and public buildings, shops and houses standing among gardens, produces a rural effect and makes the observer fancy that he is looking upon a large and finely-built country village. I have never seen a capital which seemed less like a city, or a city which had so pleasant reminders of the country. The river is half a mile wide here and the banks are too flat to be picturesque. Fish of various kinds abound in the river. Sturgeon are specially plentiful. This fish used to be prized by royalty in England; it is not considered a delicacy here. Yet great zeal is shown in catching sturgeon because the business is profitable. I visited a station where four men were engaged in fishing. They had caught twenty fish within twenty-four hours; all these sturgeon were large, one of them measured six feet in length. The price paid for each, irrespective of size, is fifty cents. I was told that, when the fish reached Boston, which was their destination, they would fetch five dollars each. It is strange that the New Brunswickers have no relish for the fish, because it is good, though rather substantial eating. But a prejudice such as they entertain cannot be removed by argument, any more than the prejudice of the Irish people against rabbits and of the Scottish people against eels.

Moncton takes rank, after the Capital and St. John, as the most rising New Brunswick town. It is the headquarters of the Intercolonial Railway and the junction where the trains meet which run between Halifax and St. John and Halifax and Quebec. While St. John is situated not far from the mouth of the Bay of Fundy, Moncton is at the head of that extraordinary sheet of water which, as the tide flows and ebbs, rises and falls in certain places as much as sixty feet. So far from the sea as Moncton, the difference between low and high water is thirty feet, and the contrast is most striking between the vast expanse of almost dry ground when the tide is out and the area of water where the largest ships can float when the tide is at its height. The phenomena called the "bore," which is occasionally seen on the Severn, is a common occurrence at this part of the Bay of Fundy.

A few years ago Moncton was a straggling and quiet village. The old and the new are easily distinguishable, the town having recently grown in the opposite direction to that which it followed in its early days. When the 600 acres within which it stands are covered with buildings the place will have an imposing appearance, and the main street, which is a mile long, will not seem so different from the other streets. As the centre of a large agricultural district, Moncton has long been a place where much business was transacted and this accounts for the number of stores appearing to be far in excess of what the inhabitants could support. The articles on sale in some of these stores are very varied. On a notice-board outside one of them a list of the goods kept began with Bibles and Prayer Books and ended with newspapers, but did not include the potatoes, turnips, cabbages and other vegetables which were the chief things to be seen indoors.

Late in the evening of the first day I spent in Moncton, I gazed upon a sight grander than any which I had beheld elsewhere, unless I except a fire in the woods on the bank of the St. John River. I have seen a prairie ablaze and I have looked with wonder at the "tules" or gigantic bulrushes such as grow on the banks of the Nile, burning as far as the eye could reach along the left bank of the Sacramento River in California, but this was the first time that I beheld the conflagration of a forest. At first the fire seemed trifling, but the flames gradually rose in angry shape and spread in serried masses as tree after tree succumbed to the effects of an element which, in this case, was really a devouring one. The march of the fire was marked next morning by a space through the forest as clearly defined as if it had been wrought by machinery, and by hundreds of blackened trees which would never bud again. The sight of these bare and lifeless poles is a common one here; the poles are termed " ram-pikes." They are utterly useless, being valueless as timber and merely cumbering the ground. The people of Moncton thought nothing of a sight which impressed me greatly. They care no more about the loss of a part of a forest by fire than the inhabitants of a coal district care about the ignition and loss of a pile of waste coal at the pit's mouth. One of them, however, sympathized with me. He had left Ireland thirty years ago and he had prospered in New Brunswick, and he expressed his opinion that the folks in the old country would naturally regard the destruction of so much valuable timber as a serious calamity; adding that wood was too plentiful and cheap in New Brunswick to be sufficiently valued. But the day is at hand when even the forests of this Province will cease to be sources of wealth and to be regarded as practically inexhaustible. The area covered by primeval forest is gradually becoming cleared. Where young trees are allowed to grow they do not furnish timber equal in value to that derived from the old ones. Indeed, the industry of "lumbering" which used to be a leading and profitable one in this Province, as well as in the adjoining State of Maine, is growing less remunerative year after year. The day is not distant when it will have to be exchanged for that of cultivating the soil or rearing cattle and I do not hold that the exchange will be a loss. The farmer and the grazier make quite as industrious and sober citizens as "lumbermen."

The gentleman to whom I have just referred was an Irishman who has found in the Dominion a home which reconciles him to live away from his native Erin. He was a patriot in his youth who regarded O'Connell with idolatry. His affection for the land of his birth is strong enough to cause him to watch its fortunes with intense interest. He seemed, however, to entertain a sentiment akin to that which made Horace Walpole declare that he would love his country exceedingly if it were not for his countrymen. He was personally acquainted with many of the Irishmen who devote themselves in the United States to stir up strife in Ireland. Between them and the Irish in Canada there is a strong antagonism. This was shown by the murder of Darcy McGee for his opposition to Fenianism and his denunciation of Fenians. My informant was emphatic in stating that his countrymen in New Brunswick were perfectly satisfied with their lot, and his desire was that thousands, whose hearts were set upon having land of their own to cultivate and who could not attain their object in Ireland, might emigrate to that Province. No Province in Canada, nor any State in the Union is so liberal to settlers as New Brunswick. In the year 1868 an Act was passed by the Provincial Legislature empowering the Government to give free grants of 100 acres of land to a settler who paid a sum of $20 to be expended in making roads, or who gave his labour to the value of $10 for three years in succession, who built a house within two years and cultivated ten acres within three. An Act of 1872, now in force, is more liberal still. Under it an actual settler can obtain 100 acres of Crown land if a single man, and 200 acres if he be married and have two or more children, on condition that a house is built and three acres are cultivated within a year and ten acres within three years. After the house is built, the Government makes a present to the settler of $30. Moreover, he is protected against utter ruin by a law giving immunity to his property to the amount of $600, in the event of execution for debt.

It is not easy for a visitor to the city of St. John to believe that nearly the whole of it was a blackened ruin a few years ago. A vacant charred space here and there proclaims in an unmistakable fashion that a fire has swept a building away; but the general aspect of the city is that of a prosperous place which has never been devastated by fire. Most of the buildings are new, but new buildings are what one expects to see on the North American Continent. Some of them, such as the banks of Nova Scotia and New Brunswick, are effective specimens of architecture. The Custom House has an imposing aspect, resembling in several particulars the Louvre at Paris. The docks are spacious and filled with ships; it is the boast of the citizens that St. John ranks after Glasgow in the amount of its registered shipping and is, in fact, the fourth port in the Empire. Churches abound. As the city is built on a series of eminences, the Churches and the Church spires are visible at every turn. In answer to my inquiry whether St. John were not a very pious city, the landlord of the hotel in which I stayed replied that I ought not to reckon the Churches as a guide to such a conclusion, because they were largely exceeded in number by the "whisky-holes." I heard many lamentations about the prevalence of intemperance. Efforts are made to lessen it by prohibiting the sale of strong drink, in imitation of the system prevailing in the adjoining State of Maine. The struggle is carried on with a bitterness which does not edify the spectator and which cannot produce lasting good, whatever the political issue may be. My own opinion is that, if half the energy and money expended in this controversy with the effect of stirring up bad blood, were devoted to encouraging immigration the Province would gain enormously. A new industry dating from the year 1879 promises to increase the wealth of the Province. This is the exportation of sheep and cattle to England. No part of the Dominion is better adapted than New Brunswick for rearing cattle and the proximity of the sea-board is a natural advantage of the first importance. Like Nova Scotia it has been inadequately appreciated by the emigrants from the Old World; indeed these two Maritime Provinces of Canada, which are among the oldest of any, are really less known than the younger which are more remote and far more difficult of access. The emigrant who has resolved upon leaving the United Kingdom for Canada might go farther west than New Brunswick and fare worse than if he settled there.

# CHAPTER IV.

### PRINCE EDWARD ISLAND.

THE Island now called Prince Edward was known as St. Johns Island till 1800. In that year its name was changed to commemorate the sojourn of the Queen's father in British North America. Till 1770 it formed a part of the Province of Nova Scotia. In 1873 it became a Province of the Dominion of Canada. Though the smallest member of the Dominion, its area being a little in excess of 2000 square miles, it has a population of 100,000, which is proportionately larger than that of any other Canadian territory of the like extent. The situation of Prince Edward Island in the Gulf of St. Lawrence corresponds, in its relation to Canada, to that of the Isle of Wight in its relation to England. The climate is milder and more equable than on the mainland. The sea breeze tempers the summer heat, and renders the Island a pleasant place of resort during the warm season. The sea-bathing on the north side is excellent, and of late years many persons, not from Canada only, but from the United States also, take up their abode here in the summer time and enjoy a dip in the Atlantic surf.

Though the distance across the Straits of Northumberland between Cape Traverse, on the Island, and Cape Tourmentine, on the shore of New Brunswick, is 9 miles, and between the opposite end of the Island and Nova Scotia 15 miles, yet the journey over the route taken by the steamer occupies four to five hours. During the winter months communication with the mainland is maintained with difficulty, it being often an arduous feat to force a passage through the ice which fills the Straits. In spring, summer and autumn, steamers ply every other day between Point du Chene, in New Brunswick, and Summerside, the second town of importance on the south coast of the Island, and between Pictou, in Nova Scotia, and Charlottetown, the capital of the Island. When beheld from the sea on a bright day, the Island looks very beautiful. Its cliffs are as red as those of South Devon, and the combination of red rocks, dark green woods, and green fields, dotted with white houses, is very pleasing to the eye. The coast is frequently indented with bays, running far inland, and swarming with fish. Shell-fish abound. Oysters are plentiful and good. They are in great request at Halifax and other cities on the mainland. The shells are longer and the contents are larger than those of English oysters, and also than those of the " Blue Points " which are highly prized in the United States. On the other hand, they resemble English oysters in taste more than those of the United States.

The chief fishing industry is that of catching and curing mackerel, and tinning lobsters for exportation. There are nearly 50 factories in which lobster preserving is carried on, giving employment to 2000 persons. Some of the factories treat from 10,000 to 15,000 lobsters a day. It was expected that 125,000 cases, each containing 48 tins 1lb. in weight, would be exported the season of my visit. The price paid to the fishermen for every lobster delivered at the factory is half a cent, and the present shipping price of each box holding 48 tins of 1lb., is $4 25c.; in other words, nearly 43 lb. of lobster can be bought for export at a trifle over 16s. If I do not mistake, the retail price of a tin in England is 9d., so the margin between 16s. paid here and the 30s. obtained for a case in England leaves a large percentage out of which to defray incidental expenses and to gain a profit. I am told that lobster catching is forbidden by law during the month of August. The fishermen neither seem to care anything about a close time, nor to pay a willing respect to the law which decrees it. One of them told me that, in his opinion, lobsters were always in season, and that he did not believe any one knew or would ever know when they spawned. He adduced evidence to the effect that, at all periods, they presented the appearance of being in a condition to spawn. Yet there can be no doubt in the minds of rational men that lobsters can be exterminated, just as oysters have been in places, if the number taken from a given spot be in excess of the number produced.

The cultivators of the soil thrive as well on Prince Edward Island as the harvesters of the sea. Oats, potatoes, and buckwheat are the most remunerative crops. Large quantities of oats are exported to Europe. Hay is exported to the West Indies; oats, hay, eggs, fish, and other edibles are exported to Nova Scotia, New Brunswick, and Massachusetts. For several months in the year, a steamer which runs weekly between Charlottetown and Boston carries away many young islanders of both sexes, as well as the produce of the farms. The desire of the young men and women to visit Boston is as keen as the desire of young people in the rural districts of England to visit London. In both cases they consider that, when the capital of the country is reached, their fortunes are made. I asked some of the young islanders what was the special attraction of Boston. They replied that they had been told they could get high wages there. They did not know that if the wages they received were higher than those obtainable in the island, the price of what they had to buy was higher also. Besides, they had the inducement of being able to make the experiment at the low cost of $8, and they were sanguine that they would have no reason to regret the change. It was the change of life which most of them desired. They could not complain of anything save the monotony of existence; the Island seemed far too contracted a world to them.

Prince Edward Island has an established reputation for producing excellent potatoes. Neither in size nor quality can any potatoes be found of a superior kind. As many as three and a half million bushels are produced in a single year. But the main difficulty is to find a market for this useful and abundant article of food. A year ago it was possible to buy a bushel of potatoes for 10 cents. At the time of my visit the price had risen to 15 cents, though 25 is the price at which the seller obtains a handsome profit. Even at 25 cents, or one shilling, the price is extremely low from an English point of view, seeing that one penny a pound is accounted cheap by the purchasers of potatoes by retail. A bushel which sells in the Island for one shilling sterling would thus command five shillings in the London market. Last year, three steamers were freighted with potatoes from Prince Edward Island to England, but the result, unfortunately, was disastrous to the exporters. Whether the cause was imperfect packing or some other mistake, certain it is that the potatoes arrived at their destination in so bad a condition that the parties who engaged in the venture lost money. I understand that the attempt will be renewed, and I hope that the issue may be more satisfactory.

The first settlement of this Island on an extensive scale took place shortly after the beginning of the present century. It is not generally known, I think, that among the few sensible measures of Mr. Addington's much ridiculed Administration was one for encouraging settlers to make Prince Edward Island their home. Lord Selkirk stirred Mr. Addington to move in this matter. It was Lord Selkirk's desire to divert the stream of emigration to the British possessions in North America. He induced 800 Highlanders to proceed to the Island in 1803.

They prospered exceedingly. The colony would have had many accessions had not war again broken out in Europe. When the war was drawing to a close in 1812, Lord Selkirk had set his heart upon what is now the Province of Manitoba, as the most eligible place for settlement; he had become chairman of the Hudson Bay Company and he had bought a large tract of land in the North-west. Other Scottish families emigrated to the Island. The two parties were divided into hostile camps on the question of religious worship, the one being attached to the Roman Catholic form, and the other preferring the Presbyterian. Down to the present day there is enmity between the descendants of the two sets of immigrants from Scotland. The branch of the Church of England in the Island has also many adherents. The tendency in the Episcopal Church is towards the extreme form of Ritualism.

There is now an end to the conflict which raged for a century between the tillers and proprietors of the soil in Prince Edward Island. From the date of its cession to England in 1763 down to 1875, statesmen were perplexed with a "land question" there. At the outset the best mode in which to dispose of the land had received great consideration. It was surveyed in 1766; two years before it had been granted to

Lord Egmont who was enamoured of that feudal system which, even in his day, was accounted foolishness by many peers. His scheme was to divide the Island into fifty baronies; each baron was to erect a castle with a moat and drawbridge in genuine mediæval fashion, he was to maintain a certain number of men-at-arms and do suit and service to the Lord Paramount. Upon the merchants of London hearing that the king had granted this Island to Lord Egmont they valued the gift at half a million sterling. When his scheme for dealing with it was published, the public laughed at him and doubted whether he possessed his senses as well as an island. Sancho Panza could not have made a more absurd proposition about the Island of Barataria.

Finding that he could not turn his grant to account Lord Egmont relinquished it, and the Board of Trade and Plantations devised a scheme of their own. According to this scheme, the Island was divided into 67 townships of 20,000 acres each; the proprietor of each township was to find a settler for every 200 acres, within ten years after entering into possession, and to pay a sum varying from six to two shillings yearly for each 100 acres held by him. The applicants for the land were so many, being far in excess of the quantity to be allotted, that it was resolved to put up the whole as prizes in a lottery, subdividing the townships into lots of a half or a third. The prize-holders became the proprietors of the Island, with the exception of two townships which had been reserved for the use of a fishing company. In a single day of the year 1767, 1,360,000 acres of land were appropriated to persons not many of whom had the intention either of settling on the Island or of inducing others to do so. The prizes were sold for cash; many fetched as much as 1000*l.* at first; but, the supply continuing, they ceased to have any value in the market.

Very few of the proprietors fulfilled the conditions under which they obtained their lands. In only ten townships were the conditions complied with as to settling one person for every 200 acres, before the expiry of the time when the lands were to be forfeited in the event of all the conditions not being fulfilled. The quit rents remained unpaid. These proprietors were defaulters to the Crown and at the same time exacting landlords. They declined to pay the rents for which they held their lands, but they insisted upon rents being paid to them by the tenants to whom they leased the lands. The scandal was so glaring that as far back as 1770 an agitation began in the Island for the forfeiture of estates to which the holders had ceased to enjoy an indisputable title. Year after year the dissatisfaction waxed stronger. Nothing of a decisive kind was accomplished till 1853 when the Provincial Legislature passed an Act authorizing the Government to purchase such estates as might be offered for sale and to resell them, in portions, to the tenants. Between 1854 and 1871, thirteen estates, comprising 457,260 acres, were bought by the Commissioner of Crown Lands, acting for the Government, at a cost of $518,294. In every case of re-sale the sum obtained for each acre was larger than that paid, so that the redistribution of the estates was profitable to the Government as well as satisfactory to both tenants and landlords. The Act was permissive only. Like all permissive legislation this attempt to settle the "land question" was fundamentally weak. The best landlords readily disposed of their property, the worst or the most useless refused to come to terms. Thus the agitation throughout the Island did not abate and the call for a drastic measure grew louder and more general.

In 1860 another attempt was made to effect a settlement of the popular grievances by appointing a Commission to devise and enforce a measure for converting leasehold into freehold estates. The Commissioners consisted of the Hon. J. H.

Gray of New Brunswick, nominated by the British Government; the Hon. Joseph Howe of Nova Scotia, nominated by the Legislature of Prince Edward Island, and the Hon. J. W. Ritchie of Halifax, nominated by the proprietors. A Provincial Act was passed giving the force of law to the Commissioners' award. On the award being published the proprietors raised a technical objection to the manner in which provision was made for valuing the land. The Commissioners had devolved the duty of valuing the land upon other persons, whereas they ought to have discharged it themselves. Hence it was that their Report and award which the Duke of Newcastle, then Secretary of State for the Colonies, pronounced " able and impartial " were invalidated and their labour led to no result. The people throughout the Island regarded this conduct on the part of the proprietors as betokening bad faith and a determination to thwart a thorough and enduring settlement. Accordingly the agitation increased in strength and the demands of the tenants became more extreme as well as more menacing to social order. A " Tenant's League " was formed with the avowed purpose of resisting the payment of rents. The civil power, not being able to make head against the opposition to authority, a military force was despatched from Halifax to aid in upholding and enforcing the law. Rents were collected at the point of the bayonet; unless overwhelming force backed the demand, they were withheld. This lamentable and discreditable state of things lasted from 1865 till 1875 when the Land Purchase Act was passed. Under this Act the proprietor of any piece of land, or pieces of land amounting in the aggregate to 500 acres, who was in the receipt of rents, could be compelled to have his interest valued by a Commission and to have his property transferred to the Commissioner of Public Lands in exchange for the price fixed by the Commission and paid to him. No proprietor who cultivated his own land was affected by the Act, provided his estate did not exceed 1000 acres. The opposition of the proprietors to this Act was pertinacious and vehement. A petition to the Crown praying that the Act might be disallowed, set forth that the Act embodied " a most unconstitutional principle," that it was utterly " destructive to the rights and property " of the petitioners, that it reproduced to a considerable extent in one provision " the worst features of the Star Chamber," that it was an " act of open and sweeping confiscation " directed against persons " whose only crime was to possess land in Prince Edward Island." However, the Act was put in force, the Commission over which Mr. Childers presided as representative of the Dominion of Canada, held its sittings and made its awards. Cases of discontent were common, as was to be expected when the persons affected objected to the whole proceedings; but cases of real hardship were rare and the Island has ceased to be the theatre of angry disputes respecting the tenure and treatment of land.

The proprietors' loss has been the Island's gain. I found general satisfaction as to the result. I learnt also that, since the settlement of the land question and the transformation of leasehold into freehold properties the area of land under cultivation has largely increased and that this salutary process is continuing. I have since read the last report of Mr. Donald Ferguson, the Land Commissioner, which contains minute and satisfactory details as to the working of the Act. The following extract is instructive; the passage which I print in italics I consider to be specially deserving of attention:—
"The sums received at this office during the years 1877, 1878, and 1879 in payment of instalments, and interest on purchase-money, amount to $177,878 76c. A much larger sum would no doubt have been received were it not for the great depression in trade existing during that period, causing a decline in the prices usually received

for agricultural products. Whilst some of the tenants are somewhat slow in meeting their instalments as they fall due, *the majority are making commendable efforts in that direction, and the public sentiment in the Colony will sustain the Department of Public Lands in firmly but prudently enforcing payment of the balances remaining unpaid by the tenants."*

A narrow guage railway, which runs from one end of the Island to the other, is of great service in developing its agricultural resources. Farmers can get their produce carried quickly and cheaply to the port of shipment. The railway is not a very pleasant one to travel on. There are no mountains in the Island, yet there are plenty of undulations and, as the line is carried up one slope and down another and round sharp curves, the consequence is that the trains oscillate and jar to a great extent. A serious accident which occurred shortly before I journeyed on the railway, was attributed to the imperfect condition of the permanent way and the Dominion Government, who manage the line, were bitterly denounced for this by their political opponents. Their political supporters were quite as ready to maintain that the Government deserved thanks for having kept the line in excellent condition. I could not find evidence of any other fault save that of running trains at too great a speed over dangerous curves and high gradients.

Shipbuilding used to be the great industry of this Island. As many as 100 vessels were on the stocks at one time in the several yards, some being of 1000 tons burden. The demand for wooden vessels having fallen off, the Islanders are the losers. At Summerside, I saw but one small vessel on the stocks; it was thought a subject of congratulatory notice in the newspapers that another of 600 tons, which was about to be built, would give employment to some of the ship-wrights who had been for some time in enforced idleness. Timber of the best quality is so abundant, labour is so plentiful and there are so many facilities here for supplying wooden vessels of the highest class at the lowest price that, should a demand for them spring up again, the Islanders will have busy times. I fancy, however, that wooden hulls are destined to diminish in number and to be superseded by iron ones.

Summerside, the second largest town in the Island, is in communication by steamer with Point du Chene, in New Brunswick. The population is not much more than 3000. An attempt to make it a place of resort for summer tourists has failed for the present. This consisted in building a palatial hotel, called the Island Park

Hotel, on an island in the Bay. The Island covers 200 acres and the grounds in which the hotel stands are beautifully laid out; a steam ferry keeps up communication between the hotel and Summerside. For a time the 600 rooms in the hotel were filled, but the visitors gradually departed without any intimation that they would return. The result has been a heavy loss to the proprietor of the hotel, which was closed when I saw it. Everything seemed in its favour. The situation was lovely; a pleasanter spot on which to spend a few days or weeks it would be hard to find. But the sojourner in the Island Park Hotel found that it was less of a paradise than might have been supposed. I was told that the Island produces mosquitoes of a specially vicious and persevering character, and that these mosquitoes did not rest till they had made the hotel too hot for its occupants. I have known cases of eyes being closed owing to mosquito stings, but I never before heard of mosquitoes shutting up a hotel. It is certain that the hotel was a failure and it is possible that the mosquitoes were unjustly blamed for a misfortune which might have been due to other causes. I did not sojourn on the Island where the hotel stands; I cannot write from personal knowledge of its character as the hunting-ground for sanguinary insects, but I can say that I was untroubled by mosquitoes in Prince Edward Island.

Charlottetown, the Capital, is the largest city in the Island and even it does not contain more than 10,000 inhabitants. Its situation is admirable, being built on a rising ground at the bottom of Hillsborough Bay and at the confluence of the rivers Hillsborough, York, and Elliot. From the upper part of the city the prospect is charming; in the distance are the hills of Nova Scotia, between them and the Island lie the Straits of Northumberland and many sheets of water filling irregular indentations in the shore, as well as many small islands or promontories covered with trees. There are several important buildings in Charlottetown, the principal one being the Colonial Building, where the Government officials and the Legislature are accommodated. The suburbs contain neat villas, surrounded with flower-gardens tastefully laid out and well kept. In traversing this Island and visiting the private houses and living in the hotels, one is pleasantly reminded of the Old World; there is not much bustle and there is much more comfort. Times do not appear to have changed materially since the Island was divided into three counties, Kings, Queens and Princes, and since the chief streets of its capital were traced and named

Kent, Dorchester, Grafton, Queen and Great George. The conductors of the newspapers are less disposed than the other Prince Edward Islanders to take life easily and quietly. They display much energy and fertility in personal attack and recrimination. The newspapers often contain specimens of the style of journalism typified by the *Eatanswill Gazette*. Professional politicians, who are as active and unpopular here as they are in other parts of North America, frequently make public statements about each other's motives and conduct which the charitable stranger must hope are grossly exaggerated, if not wholly unfounded.

Though the smallest Province of Canada, this one is not the least worthy of a visit. The future of the Island will probably resemble its past in all respects save the controversy concerning the land question, and also in the advance in wealth and population going on at an accelerated speed. It is possible that coal exists at a great depth, and it is known that a small quantity of iron ore exists, but the only natural wealth of the Island is in the trees which still remain and show how the whole country looked when it was entirely covered with forest, in the soil which is very fertile, in the game which is very plentiful and in the fish which swarm around the Island and fill its many rivers.

## Governor John Ready's Administration.

During several years of its early history, complaints were made as to the injury wrought by the rapacity and tyranny of the Governors sent from England. One of them, Governor Smith, was actually removed in 1813 for misconduct, in deference to the strong complaints of the inhabitants. Since the Island has enjoyed responsible government, that is since 1851, its rulers have not had the power, even if inspired with a wish to do, mischief. The pleasantest memories of bygone days are associated with Governor John Ready who displayed a benevolent disposition and a sincere desire to promote the welfare of the people. It was in 1827, during his Administration, that the first Census was taken, the population being found to number 23,266. At the beginning of the century the number was 5000. The census of 1871 showed that the population had increased to 94,021; it is estimated that about 15,000 have been added to the people during the last ten years. These statistics prove a steady increase in population and there is no apparent reason why the progress should be speedily arrested.

After visiting the Maritime Provinces of Canada, I was struck with the advantage which they would derive from a legislative union. Before the Confederation Act of 1867 was passed, it had been proposed to confederate the Maritime Provinces, but the jealousy and opposition of each was too great to be surmounted. Since becoming Provinces of the Dominion, complaints are frequently made that they do not exercise so much influence at Ottawa as the Provinces of Quebec and Ontario. This grievance would be mitigated or removed if they joined their forces and acted as a unit. Their interests are identical; a single Provincial Legislature could provide for their local affairs, while as a united body, they would command greater respect in the Dominion Parliament. Home rule has its advantages; but, when three legislatures exist in a population of 800,000, the cost of home rule is greater than the benefit. Whether the Maritime Provinces make this change or whether they remain as they are, they will be the better appreciated in Europe, the more they are known, and the tourist who desires to see new places will find a trip through them both enjoyable and instructive. The time wasted by ambitious travellers in aimless journeys round the world and in describing what they had imperfectly seen and understood, would be more advantageously expended, while literature might have a lesser quantity of rubbish added to it, if they leisurely traversed and truthfully described the Maritime Provinces of Canada.

# CHAPTER V.

### INTERCOLONIAL, GRAND TRUNK, AND NORTHERN RAILWAYS.

In 1838 the Earl of Durham strongly urged the British Government to construct a railway between Halifax and Quebec. In 1876 the Intercolonial Railway was completed and opened for traffic. When passengers were first enabled in 1869 to travel by rail from New York to San Francisco, they rejoiced that this had been rendered possible. It was not remembered that the construction of a Pacific Railway was advocated by John Plumbe in 1836. The rule is for a great national undertaking to be delayed at least thirty years longer than is absolutely necessary. A generation often passes away before the project of a far-seeing man is carried into effect by the persons whom he has converted to his views and who, when they see the feasibility and success of the undertaking are ready enough to appropriate the credit which is his due.

The first objection made to the Intercolonial Railway, while it was still the subject of consideration, was that it could not be constructed; the second was that, if constructed, traffic over it would be suspended during the winter months; the third and, in the opinion of most persons, the conclusive one was that, even if constructed, it could not possibly pay. The objections made in the United States to the Pacific Railway were of the same character and were equally conclusive. Engineering skill has overcome all natural obstacles in both cases. The trains on both lines run with regularity all the year round, and both are successful railway undertakings. With regard to all such undertakings as great trunk railways or interoceanic canals, the prophecies of failure are the only things connected with them which usually remain unfulfilled.

The Intercolonial Railway is the most palpable result of Canadian Confederation. At a meeting held at Quebec in 1864 of the delegates from the Provinces which first constituted the Dominion of Canada it was resolved, and this resolution was afterwards incorporated in the Imperial Act creating the Dominion, that " the general government shall secure, without delay, the completion of the Intercolonial Railway from Rivière du Loup, through New Brunswick, to Truro, in Nova Scotia." In accordance with this resolution and with a capital of 3,000,000*l.* raised under Imperial guarantee, the construction of the railway was begun in 1869. Several surveys and plans for a railway had been made at an earlier day. The first scheme referred to a line, surveyed by Major Yule, R.E., which was to run from St. Andrew's in New Brunswick to Quebec and which a joint-stock Company was to construct with the sanction of the British Government. The International dispute as to the boundary between New Brunswick and the State of Maine caused the postponement of this undertaking, and the Ashburton treaty under which certain territory, claimed and occupied by Great Britain, was ceded to the United States, caused the project to be abandoned. Several other plans for constructing a railway from the sea-board to Quebec through British territory were successively mooted, matured and laid aside. The great work was ultimately begun and completed, without half the difficulty which was expected and with more advantage to those primarily affected than had been imagined or foretold.

Though not so gigantic a work as the Pacific Railway from Omaha to San Francisco, it is yet no trifling display of engineering capacity. Its total length, including branches to Pictou and Shediac, is 713 miles. A more substantial line of rail is not to be found anywhere. The permanent way is in admirable condition; the rails are of steel; the bridges are of stone or iron; the engines and carriages are made of the best materials and on the latest models in the Government workshops at Moncton. It is indisputable that the snowfall is very heavy and the cold is intense in winter throughout much of the country through which the line runs. A part of it passes along a tract 743 feet above the sea level. In the Metapedia Valley the weather is frequently severe, yet the detention of a train owing to bad weather is rarer than in the Highlands of Scotland. This is largely due to the careful provision which has been made for all contingencies. Wherever the snow is likely to drift and bar the passage of a train, fences have been erected to keep it off the line; where it might fill up a cutting, snow sheds have been built; one of these sheds, which is upwards of a mile in length, cost $1,500,000. In this case, however, the outlay has proved to be judicious economy. Only a short section of the line has baffled the efforts of the engineers to render it perfectly free from risk or trouble; this consists of a vast slope composed of clay down which, in the spring-time, a heavy mass sometimes slides and sweeps rails and everything else before it. Various remedies have been tried in vain. As the clay is of excellent quality and bricks are in demand, it might serve a double purpose to erect a brick-making machine and thus turn the erratic clay to useful account.

During my visit to Moncton, the headquarters of the Railway, I had the privilege of inspecting the Company's workshops and offices under the guidance of Mr. Bruce, the Chief Clerk, who was in temporary charge during the absence of Mr. Pottinger, the Government Superintendent, to whom I had an introduction. I was impressed with the business-like way in which everything was arranged and executed. The workshops are on a large scale, consisting of three huge buildings which cover 70 acres; as many as 2000 men being employed when the demand for making or repairing cars and locomotives is at its height. A proof of the care with which the line is managed is the fact that carefully compiled Meteorological tables are kept at each station and forwarded at regular intervals to the head office, where they are filed for reference. This may seem superfluous, yet it is an eminently sensible as well as a practical arrangement. Should the Manager be called upon to make compensation for damage to goods in course of transit, it may happen that the

## Intercolonial Railway.

damage is entirely due to excessive heat or excessive cold or to a condition of the weather which exonerates the railway authorities from blame and from any liability to pay damages. By referring to the Meteorological tables on the given day at the place in question, the state of the weather can be ascertained and thus a dispute may be averted or settled.

There can be no doubt that the Intercolonial Railway is excellently constructed and admirably managed. The Chief Clerk, Mr. Bruce, who readily afforded me all the information I desired and displayed a courtesy which I heartily acknowledge, and Mr. Pottinger, the Superintendent, whose praise I heard from many mouths and whose ability is demonstrated by his success, evidently do their duty without reproach. Yet I am not convinced that a great railway should be a Government undertaking. The temptation to appoint or promote railway officers for party services rather than for personal merit is hard to resist and it is not easy to satisfy the public that Government patronage is uninfluenced by political considerations. Whenever this line is a paying property the Canadian Government would show wisdom in leasing it for a term of years. They would then be able to count upon an annual return without running any risk. Hitherto the working expenses have been in excess of the receipts, but the days of deficits appear to be numbered. The rate of increase has been rapid and, with one exception, continuous. In 1876-7 the deficit was $307,000; in 1877-8, it was $232,000; in 1878-9, it was $547,867; in 1879-80, it fell to $97,131. A profit has accrued at the time I write. This is the manner in which the prediction has been justified that the Intercolonial would never earn enough wherewith to pay for the grease on the axles of the wheels.

The Intercolonial Railway is not only an invaluable means of intercommunication between the Maritime and mid-Provinces of Canada, but it offers many attractions to tourists. From Halifax to Quebec the distance is 686 miles. After leaving Halifax the scenery begins to attract the beholder, nothing can be more charming than the chain of lakes with wooded islands nor can anything be more weird than the tract of country strewn with boulders. About thirty miles along the way the Gold quartz mining district is reached. Ten miles further on is Shubenacadie on a river of that name which divides Nova Scotia into two parts and abounds in shad and salmon. I was told that the sunsets at Shubenacadie were gorgeous in the extreme. The statement was verified in my own experience; never have I seen sunsets elsewhere that presented so many marvellous and brilliant effects. Truro, a refreshment station, was a small village before the railway was made; now it is a town of 5000 inhabitants. It is surrounded by meadows and it has the benefit of the ocean breeze from the Bay of Fundy. At Londonderry, a station further on, shipbuilding is the chief industry. Here the Acadian Charcoal Iron Company's works are situated; these works have been acquired by English capitalists. The outlay upon them has been 300,000$l$. and they are expected to yield, when in full operation, 20,000 tons of pig iron annually. The railway runs through the small settlement of Ishgonish, where rabbits are as plentiful as at Ostend. A local firm catches and tins these rabbits and exports them to England. The tins are labelled "Preserved Hare." Purchasers of Nova Scotia preserved hare ought to see that the contents of the tins tally with the label. The course of the line over the Cobequid Hills is very picturesque, the elevation reached being 600 feet, and the view both far and near being exceedingly beautiful. Where the level country is gained lies the village of Oxford; which is noted for its manufactures of carpenters' tools and wooden boxes. After entering the Province of New Brunswick, the most notable place on the line is Dorchester on the left bank

of the Peticodiac River. Near this place a mineral
called "jet coal" is found in large quantities.  It
is as rich in gas as cannel coal.  I pass over
Moncton which I have already described and
name Newcastle as next in order of note.  It is
the most important business place in New Brunswick after St. John.  Like St. John it has been
swept away by fire and rebuilt in a more attractive style though not a more substantial manner,
wood being principally used instead of stone which
is quite as abundant and nearly as cheap.  The
Miramichi river on which it is situated is one
of the largest in the Province, being 220 miles
long and having a width of 9 miles at its mouth.
At Bathurst the sightseer, as well as the angler,
will be repaid should he visit the Grand Falls on
the Nequissiquit River.  These Falls are 140 feet
in height, and are sublime specimens of natural
scenery.  On the banks of another river, the Tête-à-Gauche, is to be found the curious Wax-yielding
plant, *Myra Conifera;* candles made from this
wax are commonly used in the locality.  Campbellton, which is 372 miles from Halifax is a place
well known to the passengers who leave by the
night express on Saturday, as they have to remain
here all Sunday, the running of trains being forbidden on Sunday in Canada.  The attractions of
Campbellton, which greatly resemble those of the

town in Scotland after which it was named, would be more appreciated if they were not seen under compulsion. From this point to Metapedia the first village in the Province of Quebec, the scenery is diversified and the places at which the tourist might halt are many. No finer fishing can be had anywhere than in the Restigouche and Metapedia Rivers; the valleys of both streams abound with game while the scenery is on as vast and imposing a scale as in the Alps, while it has at times all the soft effects which enchant the traveller in the Pyrenees. A pretty place in the Metapedia Valley bears the unpronounceable name of Assametquaghan. Shortly after this valley is left behind, the line nears the St. Lawrence, and runs at no great distance from it for upwards of 200 miles till entering the terminus at Point Levi opposite Quebec. Here the Intercolonial ends and the Grand Trunk begins. In the latter part of the journey there are many places which tempt a halt, chief among them is Cacouna the fashionable watering-place of the Dominion. Here the visitors can amuse themselves by bathing, boating, fishing and shooting. There are several large and well-managed hotels at Cacouna, which is not only a pleasant place of resort for the holiday-maker, but also enjoys the reputation of restoring health to invalids.

I journeyed over the Intercolonial from St. John to Shediac, from Pictou to Halifax and from Halifax to Quebec. A piece of pleasant personal experience on the last journey deserves mention. This consisted in forming the acquaintance of Mr. Justice Henry, a Judge of the Supreme Court of Canada. He is a native of Nova Scotia and took a leading part in the affairs of that Province. He was an earnest advocate of the Intercolonial Railway and of the Canadian Confederation. In addition to being an active and a respected politician, he distinguished himself as a law reformer; it was at his suggestion and under his guidance that the Statutes of his native Province were revised, a work which was praised in the House of Lords by Lord Campbell, then Lord Chancellor. The reforms in legal procedure introduced by him are vast improvements on the old state of things. At a dinner given in his honour by the Bar of Nova Scotia in 1876, after his appointment as Justice of the Supreme Court and before his departure for Ottawa, the Lieutenant-Governor, Mr. Archibald, said " It is fair to say that on our smaller scale Mr. Justice Henry has had the honour of initiating in this Province something in the same line of policy which has lately been carried out in England. If his bill did not succeed at once, it, at all events, entitles him to be considered as one of the earliest and oldest advocates in this country of a policy on the subject of judicial tribunals, which has, after a long struggle, prevailed in the Mother country." I was gratified to learn from Mr. Justice Henry that the Canadian Supreme Court is working satisfactorily and fully attaining the objects of its originators. The cost of litigation is reduced, owing to appeals to the Privy Council occurring in exceptional cases only. The existence of the Supreme Court adds to, while gratifying national feeling. in Canada. I have had the good fortune to become acquainted with several Canadian Judges and I have been impressed not only with their professional attainments, but with their readiness to adapt themselves to changes of every kind and with their power of dealing with all matters as men of the world as well as trained lawyers. Among them Mr. Justice Henry is not the least notable.

## II.

The Grand Trunk Railway of Canada is a sadly familiar name in many an English household. When the line was projected its shares and bonds were considered so good and safe an investment that thrifty parents bought them as a provision for their wives and children. During its construction the interest on the bonds was punctually paid. It is now difficult to credit that the Fourth Preference Bonds were once quoted at upwards of 70*l.* each in the Stock Exchange official list. After the opening of the Victoria Bridge, when the interest on the bonds was to be paid out of earnings, many an English family was reduced to poverty, no surplus having accrued wherewith to meet the interest on all the bonds and to divide something among the shareholders. Writing on "Railways; their Cost and Profits" in the *Westminster Review* for October 1862, I stated that the Grand Trunk Railway was perhaps the most unsuccessful undertaking of the time: "it has been made fifty years too soon for profit, but not a day too soon for the Province." This prediction has as good a prospect of being verified as any prediction about the future of a railway. The receipts are now increasing so largely that bondholders who despaired of their lot are now receiving a return, and the case of the shareholders has ceased to be absolutely hopeless. This pleasing transformation is due, both to the progressive improvement in traffic, and to the great organizing and administrative ability of the General Manager, Mr. Hickson, whose policy has been ably carried into effect by his assistant Mr. Drinkwater and a well-selected and an efficient staff.

The traveller bound West from the city of Quebec can now journey over the Grand Trunk as far as Chicago. By securing a direct through line to the great city of Illinois, the Manager and Directors of the Grand Trunk have displayed as much judgment as boldness. Moreover, the Intercolonial acts as a feeder to their line, so that the connexion by rail is unbroken between Halifax on the Atlantic and Chicago on Lake Michigan.

A feeder to the Grand Trunk of great value is now in course of construction. It starts from Sherbrooke and runs through New Brunswick till it joins the railway in that Province which now runs to St. John. The saving in distance between the seaboard and Montreal over this line will be 200 miles, and the result may be to make St. John a still more dangerous rival to Halifax. It is possible also that the Intercolonial may be injuriously affected, yet of this I am very doubtful. The local traffic on the Intercolonial will not be diminished, and this is quite as remunerative as the through traffic. Indeed, there is ample room for both lines. When this new route is open the Grand Trunk will have three termini on the Atlantic, one at Portland in Maine, a second at Halifax in Nova Scotia and a third at St. John in New Brunswick. When the Canadian Pacific Railway is finished, the Grand Trunk will form an important and profitable link in the iron road which will then pass across British Territory from the Atlantic to the Pacific oceans.

It is eleven years since I first travelled over the Grand Trunk Railway; on my last journey I could scarcely fancy that the line was the same, so complete had been the improvement in the interval. At the date of my earliest trip over the Grand Trunk, the chance of arriving at the appointed hour was very slight; the probability of a breakdown, if not of a serious accident, being very great, the oscillation and jumping of the cars being intolerable. Now, the trains run with remarkable punctuality and with a smoothness equal to that on the best railway in England or elsewhere; accidents have happily become very rare. It seems to me that there is as much goods and passenger traffic on the line as can be accommodated; the pressure on the rolling stock is specially severe between Montreal and Toronto. Another line of rails may yet have to be added between these two places. I think, however, that the struggles of the Grand Trunk as a commercial undertaking are nearing their close and that the long expected period of prosperity is about to begin. Everything that can be done by skilful management to make the line remunerative has been carefully attended to, and the shareholders may yet find that their patience has not been tried in vain, and that the sanguine expectations which they once cherished about future profits were premature rather than baseless.

## III.

While the Grand Trunk runs west beyond Toronto, another line, the Northern, running in a north-westerly direction, connects that city with Collingwood on Georgian Bay. The distance between the two places is 95 miles. At Allandale a branch runs to the Muskoka district, that picturesque region of wood and water which bears many resemblances to the Highlands of Scotland. The total length of the Northern with its branches is 167 miles. It has been under the management of Colonel Cumberland since 1859. Before his advent, the prospect of the line becoming remunerative was very slight. A great change for the better has now taken place, the vigour and ability of Colonel Cumberland having altered the prospects of the railway. Not only is the line in an admirable state for transporting goods and passengers, but its stations are models of neatness and good taste. The sight of a pretty garden at a station is common enough in England, but it is so rare in Canada and the United States that the flowers, grass and shrubbery at the stations on the Northern Railway impress a stranger as exceedingly effective.

The country through which the Northern Railway runs after leaving Toronto is well adapted for farming. The Vale of Aurora is a district in which good grain is grown and horses and sheep of the best kinds are reared. Beyond the village of Aurora is Newmarket which is noted for manufactures. Half-way between Toronto and Collingwood is the Holland River Marsh, a spot where snipe and wild duck abound and where there is also excellent fishing. At Allandale, the junction for the Muskoka branch, the prospect is lovely. This place and Barrie are on Kempenfeldt Bay in Lake Simcoe. This Lake as well as the Lakes in the Muskoka district are not like the huge inland seas which entirely upset the ideas of Lakes formed by visitors to the north of England, the Highlands of Scotland and to Switzerland. The sheets of water in this part of Canada while seldom too vast to be embraced at a single glance, are exquisite in their surroundings.

It is fifteen years since the Muskoka district was thrown open for settlement and free grants of land were made to those persons who should fix their homes there. The influx of settlers has been considerable; the inhabitants numbered 300 in 1861; they now number about 10,000. Many persons have been disappointed because the land is of small value for the agriculturist, though furnishing a beautiful prospect to the tourist. The settler naturally prefers fine soil to fine scenery. Moreover, the country was in a wild state when the first settlers went thither and was not so easily farmed as in the west, where the prairie is ready for the plough. But the early failures of a few have been the exceptions and the country is now becoming filled with industrious and thriving families. Year after year it is growing in favour as a place of summer resort, being to Ontario what the Highlands are to England. All this brings traffic to the Northern Railway.

Collingwood is the most important station on the line, being the place of departure and arrival of the steamers which ply between this town and Duluth at the head of Lake Superior. Other lines of steamers run between Collingwood and Chicago. As the West becomes more populous and the surplus of products increases in amount, the trade on the Northern Lakes must grow in a corresponding ratio and this increase will add more traffic to the Northern Railway. It stands fourth, in the extent of its traffic, among Canadian lines of rail. As the line whereby north-western

Ontario will be developed and which will profit, in turn, by such development, it stands first. Possessing a virtual monopoly of an important tract of country, the Northern should attain a high place among the most successful Canadian Railways.

# CHAPTER VI.

### ACROSS LAKE SUPERIOR.

THE traveller bound for the Canadian Far West, who crosses the Atlantic in an Allan liner, reaches Toronto by rail after landing at Halifax, Rimouski or Quebec. Unless he shall have made up his mind before leaving home as to the route which he will take in order to arrive at Manitoba, he finds at Toronto that three courses are open to him and that each has its professed advantage or special temptation. First, he may proceed to Winnipeg by rail. If he travel night and day, he is at his journey's end in three days and a half. Second, he may proceed to Sarnia on Lake Huron over the Grand Trunk Railway, embark there in a steamer for Duluth, at the head of Lake Superior, where he takes the train for Winnipeg. Third, he may proceed to Collingwood on Georgian Bay over the Northern of Canada Railway, where a steamer will carry him to Duluth whence he continues his journey as in the second case. The time occupied in the third of these cases is four days and a half, being one day shorter than by the Sarnia route and one day longer than the direct route by rail. In addition to the saving in time, the third route has the advantage over the second that the voyage is made along the North Shore of Lake Superior where the scenery is bolder and more varied than on the South. During five months out of the twelve, Lake Superior is closed to navigation; the open season begins at the end of April and closes at the end of November. As the boats were running, I determined to cross the Lake and, after careful consideration, I elected to start from Collingwood in order to enjoy the attractions of the North Shore route.

Five hours after leaving Toronto on a Thursday forenoon, I reached Collingwood and I looked for the *City of Winnipeg*, the steamer which was advertised to leave the wharf shortly after the arrival of the train. I looked in vain. The steamer did not get to Collingwood on her return trip till Saturday evening, having been detained owing to boisterous weather and having been so much injured that she had to be docked for repairs. On Sunday evening the *Frances Smith*, another steamer of the same line, reached

Collingwood and her Captain reported that he had encountered a gale on the upward trip which jeopardized the vessel's safety and did some damage to her. After being temporarily repaired, she started for Duluth on Monday night. I was not sorry to leave Collingwood, having grown tired of waiting there four days for a steamer which might appear at any moment.

In other circumstances I might have liked Collingwood better. The town is of recent date. It stands upon what was formerly a cedar swamp. Its advance in importance has been rapid. The population numbers 4000. Collingwood is admirably situated for the purposes of commerce; the greater part of Ontario's trade with the Upper Lakes must pass through it. The soil in the immediate vicinity is poor, yet certain vegetables and fruits flourish there, the yield of excellent plums being very large. Small though Collingwood be, it is yet rich enough to support two weekly newspapers and one daily. There are many attractive villas in the neighbourhood where the prosperous merchants reside. There is an Episcopalian, a Methodist and a Roman Catholic Church and two Presbyterian Churches. In the two principal hotels the traveller is housed at a very moderate charge. At one of them I

obtained a comfortable room and excellent food
for the small sum of $1 a day.

The proprietor of the hotel told me an interesting story of his struggles with fortune. Born
in the North of Ireland, he came to Canada at an
early age. He migrated to Collingwood, where
he followed the trade of a shoemaker. Being a
skilful workman he was able to save a little
money and to employ men to execute the orders
he received. He had as many as eight men in
his employment and had plenty of business when
he was obliged to suspend payment owing to the
bad debts which he made. Then he became hotel
keeper, prospered in that capacity and paid all
his old creditors in full, the sum required for the
purpose being $2500. Soon afterwards his hotel
was burnt down; it was uninsured and he lost
everything except a good name and credit. On the
strength of his credit he borrowed money, wherewith to buy the site on which his hotel had stood,
and to erect a new building. He has now paid
off all his liabilities and is independent. He
ascribes his success in life to working hard and
minding his own business. He told me that his
feeling for Ireland was as warm as ever, but that
he felt ashamed of many Irishmen. He spoke
highly of the neighbouring country as a place
where farmers can prosper. There are many

farms of 100 acres with substantial house and offices which can be bought for $7000. In several cases farms are for sale because the possessors have not inherited their fathers' virtues as well as their acres. Taking life easily and giving to pleasure the energy which ought to be expended in their fields, these young men find that they have to raise money by mortgaging their land, and are often obliged to part with the land because they cannot meet the interest on the mortgages.

The *Frances Smith* is a paddle steamer. For sea-going purposes a steamer propelled by paddles is inferior to one propelled by a screw, but the former commonly affords superior accommodation to passengers. I had a better furnished and more spacious state-room in the *Frances Smith* than is to be found on the best Atlantic liners. I cannot imagine anything more enjoyable in fine summer weather than a trip in such a steamer. But when the equinoctial gales are blowing and Lake Superior is a raging sea, a steamer like this is neither comfortable nor staunch. If the engines broke down the vessel would be at the mercy of the waves. On a screw steamer sail can be carried which might prove serviceable in the event of damage to the machinery. The voyage was tedious owing to stormy weather. Leaving Collingwood on Monday night we did not reach Duluth till the succeeding Monday morning, though we were due on the previous Thursday night. Captain Robertson, who has had seven years' experience of navigating Lake Superior, had never seen a worse season; this does not prove much, however, for the Captains of steamships always appear to think that the present bad weather is unprecedented. This is their mode of flattering passengers; the latter are rather proud of hearing that their experience of the weather is altogether exceptional and that their survival is almost miraculous. However, the Captain of the *Frances Smith* demonstrated that he considered the weather very bad, for, rather than face the gale blowing in Georgian Bay, he remained twelve hours in the sheltered harbour of Owen Sound. Another steamer which left Collingwood for Chicago soon after we started, was driven on an island in Georgian Bay and became a total wreck. The Captain of our steamer had the greater reason for caution because the boat was obviously over-laden. There were several horses and fifty head of cattle on board; cargo was piled in every spot where space could be found; ample provision seemed to have been made for causing what would have been misnamed an accident.

Though the weather was unpropitious for full

enjoyment of the scenery, yet I saw enough to lead me to concur in the praise lavished upon it. As many as ten thousand islands or islets have been counted in Georgian Bay and this figure is believed to be far under the mark. Many are wooded; they differ in shape and they give a variety to the landscape which is exceedingly charming. The steamer was a whole day threading its course among this maze of islets. Killarney on the north shore is the fourth stopping-place after leaving Collingwood; it is a village consisting of about twenty houses and a church. The land is very poor in the neighbourhood; the laurentian formation is conspicuous, the outcropping of bare rock being more frequent than patches of soil. The people are Indians and Half-Breeds who live by catching fish and gathering fruit. They had many tubs of freshly caught white fish and salmon trout and barrels of cranberries for sale, the latter costing $5 each. Specimens of Indian embroidery were in a store over which was a sign "Indian Works." As a few of the houses were new, I inferred that the village of Killarney was flourishing.

A very different impression was produced by the sight of the Bruce mines. This was once a busy settlement; now it is in decay; many of the houses are empty and the church seems falling into ruin. The copper-mines around which the settlement had gathered belong to an English Company. At one time they were very remunerative. A gentleman who had managed one of the principal mines told me that, if copper were to fetch 16$d$. a pound again all these mines would return large dividends, but that, at the present price of copper, they must be worked at a heavy loss. The works are stopped and the machinery is not only idle, but it is deteriorating rapidly. However, the English Company is so fortunate as to possess in addition to unproductive mines, 6500 acres of good farming land, for which there is a demand; the capital sunk in the mines may be partly replaced from their sale.

The Bruce mines are 307 miles from Collingwood. After leaving them the steamer enters the St. Mary's River, connecting Lake Superior with Lake Huron; it is about sixty miles long. For a great part of its course it bears no resemblance to a stream, being rather a series of shallow lakes, among which Bear Lake and St. George's Lake are the most important. At the outlet of the latter the Neebish Rapids attract attention, chiefly because the current is so much less sluggish there than at other parts. The St. Mary's River is meandering as well as shallow; at parts the space between the banks is narrow and the banks themselves are very picturesque. When I saw them, their rocky sides were not only tinted with many colours but their summits were crowned with trees glowing in the gorgeous tints of a Canadian autumn. On the northern side there is an Indian reservation whereon an Indian tribe, under the rule of Chief Francis, lives by fishing and farming. In physique the chief strikingly resembles the great Duke of Wellington and in character he is quite as shrewd. He resists all encroachments on his domain. The Quebec and Lake Superior Mining Company discovered a silver-mine to which access could be had only through the Indian reservation. Chief Francis refused to allow the Company's servants to exercise the right of way which they claimed on the technical ground that the land was unfenced. When the Indians understood the nature of the claim, they lost no time in surrounding the land with fences of the strangest and most primitive kind and thus check-mated the Company. Chief Francis stands upon his legal right, and he will neither surrender his title to the land nor sell any of it. The Canadian Government respect his title, and there is no likelihood of Chief Francis having to make any change against his will. He knows that a treaty with Indians is always scrupulously respected wherever the British flag floats.

A little way further up the river, at Sault Ste. Marie, on the Canadian side, is the Shingwauk Home established six years ago by members of the Church of England in Canada for the training of young Indian boys. Two years ago the Wawanosh Home was established for training Indian girls. There is accommodation for eighty boys and thirty girls. The Government gives a small subsidy to the Homes, but voluntary contributions are their chief support. As is common with charitable institutions these two labour under the drawback of poverty. I am assured that both have been appreciated by the Indians, who are glad to send their children to be educated and, I may add, civilized there. A little monthly paper printed at the Boys' Home called the *Algoma Missionary News and Shingwauk Journal* gives information about missionary progress among the Indians. The profits from the sale go to the support of the Home; the yearly subscription is only 35 cents. Moreover, any one who desires to support a boy or girl, including clothing, can do so by paying $75 a year. The purposes and wants of these Homes only require to be generally known for their prosperity to be assured. It is through such agencies that the Indians of Canada will not only remain peaceful dwellers in the land, but are prepared and disposed to exercise the privileges of citizenship to which they are entitled, under Canadian law, whenever they choose to comply with the requisite formalities.

On the Michigan side the land is good and well-cultivated. The most comfortable looking house and the best laid grounds belong to Mr. Church who has accumulated a fortune by making raspberry jam. He settled here when this part of the State was unpeopled by white men and he employed Indians to gather the wild raspberries which grow in profusion. He made them into jam which he forwarded for sale in the more settled and civilized parts of the United States. His jam grew into favour with the public and he became very rich.

At Sault Ste. Marie the steamer passes through a canal into Lake Superior. This canal is a fine example of engineering skill, but it will soon be superseded by a still finer example. The second canal is an admirable piece of work, every part being built of the most durable materials. Vessels drawing sixteen feet of water will be able to pass through the new canal. It is not creditable to Canada that no such canal has been made on her side of the rapids. The natural difficulties are far less there, while the advantages of a canal through Canadian territory are obvious.

As a spectacle, the Rapids are very striking.

For the distance of a mile the waters of Lake Superior rush down over shelving rocks; at intervals in the descent, islets, covered with trees, form obstacles to the hurrying waters which eddy and foam around them. In the eddies white fish lie and feed till they fall a prey to the Indian fisherman. It is nearly two centuries and a half since the Sault Ste. Marie was first visited by white men. In 1641, two Jesuit missionaries, Fathers Raymbault and Jorgues, pushed their explorations as far as this place. They then found an Indian village of two thousand persons on the spot where a small United States city now stands. For centuries the Chippewa Indians had made this a place of abode, living on the white fish that swarm in the Rapids. The mode of fishing is unlike any which I ever saw practised. Two Indians stand upright at either end of a canoe and force it up the swift running stream. One attends to keeping the canoe's head up stream while the other watches for a fish; on seeing one he scoops it out with a small net attached to a pole six feet long. The pole, with the net attached, is not easily handled on land; when a fish weighing from ten to fifteen pounds is in it, the physical exertion required to raise the net must be great. There is a knack in this as in all other feats; but it is one which none but Indians are known to acquire. The Indians get 2 cents a pound for the fish they catch, which are packed in ice and sent to Detroit. The fish caught in the Rapids are better eating than those caught above or below them, the flesh being firmer and the taste being more delicate. I never enjoyed a greater delicacy than a piece of white fish which I ate within half an hour after the fish had been swimming in the water. Another new sensation I did not covet. This consists in running the Rapids in a canoe. Adventurous and curious persons can have their desire gratified by Indians in exchange for $5. The first step is the payment which is enforced before-hand, the next is to spend a couple of minutes in breathless excitement, as the canoe spins down the foaming water, and to be drenched by the spray through which the canoe passes, the final conclusion being that the game is not worth the cost.

When one looks at these Rapids where fishing has been prosecuted in the same fashion for centuries, one is not so greatly struck with the little change in this respect which has taken place, as with the greatness of other changes. Powerful Indian tribes, whom the first white man laboured to conciliate before essaying their conversion, have passed away leaving only names behind. The Jesuit Fathers who visited this spot would have less difficulty in recognizing it again if they could return to earth, than in realizing the transformation in the position of that great French nation which they admirably represented and devotedly served in the wilds of western Canada. Few scenes in French colonial history are so memorable as that of which this place was the theatre on the 14th of June, 1671. A grand council then assembled, in which fourteen Indian tribes were represented, where the Rev. Claude Dablon, Superior of the Lake Missions, Fathers Gabriel Druillettes, Claude Alloüez, and Louis André represented the Church, and where M. Daumont de St. Lusson with fifteen of his followers represented the Government of Louis the Fourteenth. A large cross was blessed by Father Dablon and erected on a hill, while the Frenchmen, with bare heads, sang the *Vexilla Regis*. Near the cross a post was fixed in the ground and to it was fastened a metal plate on which the royal arms were engraved; the *Exaudiat* was sung and a prayer offered for the King during this part of the ceremony. Then Daumont de St. Lusson stood forth with upraised sword in one hand and a clod of earth in the other and said in a loud voice: "In the name of the most high, mighty, and renowned monarch Louis, Fourteenth of that name, most Christian King of France and Navarre, I take possession of this place, Sainte Marie du

Sant, as also of Lakes Huron and Superior, the Island of Manatoulin, and all countries, rivers, lakes, and streams contiguous and adjacent thereunto; both those which have been discovered and those which may be discovered hereafter, in all their length and breadth, bounded on the one side by the seas of the North and of the West, and on the other by the South Sea: declaring to the nations thereof that from this time forth they are vassals of his Majesty, bound to obey his laws and follow his customs: promising to them on his part all succour and protection against the incursions and invasions of their enemies: declaring to all other potentates, princes, sovereigns, states and republics,—to them and to their subjects,—that they cannot and are not to seize and settle upon any parts of the aforesaid countries, save only under the good pleasure of his most Christian Majesty, and of him who will govern on his behalf; and this on pain of incurring his resentment and the efforts of his arms. Long live the King."[1]

After the representative of the King had performed his official duty, Father Alloüez harangued the Indians about the ceremonies which they had witnessed, impressing upon them that they should worship Christ upon the Cross, and honour and obey the King, who, he told them, had no equal upon earth. Many fulsome panegyrics were passed upon Louis during his

[1] Translated and quoted by Mr. Parkman in his admirable work "The Discovery of the Great West," pp. 41-2.

lifetime, but none surpassed this one. The Indians were told that when Louis goes to war all his chiefs raise armies. "When he attacks, he is more fearful than thunder. The earth trembles, and the air and the sea are on fire from the discharge of his cannon. He has been seen in the midst of his squadrons covered with the blood of his enemies; so many of them has he put to the sword that he does not number their scalps, but merely the rivers of blood which he has caused to flow. He carries such a number of captives with him that he does not value them, but lets them go where they please, to show that he does not fear them. Nobody dares make war on him. All nations beyond the sea have sued for Peace with great submission. They come from every quarter of the globe and listen to him and admire him. It is he who decides upon the affairs of the world. What shall I say of his riches? You think yourselves very rich when you have ten or twelve sacks of corn, and hatchets, and kettles and other things of the kind. He has more cities than you have men, which are scattered over a space of more than five hundred leagues. In each city there are shops containing hatchets enough to cut all your wood, kettles enough to cook all your cariboo and sugar enough to fill all your wigwams. His house extends further than from here to the Sault, is higher than the tallest of your trees, and contains more people than the largest of your settlements ever contained."

It is doubtful whether the Indians to whom Father Alloüez recounted the feats and magnificence of the great Louis were so much impressed by the recital as they were by Lake Superior. The Lake they worshipped. It was the source of their chief food and it represented to them the might and mystery of the ocean. No other sheet of fresh water on the globe is larger or more wonderful. Its extreme length is 355 miles and its breadth 160 ; it covers an area of 32,000 square miles. The surface of the Lake is 627 feet above the sea level; parts of its bed are several hundred feet below it ; hence it is one of the deepest depressions on the earth's face. The largest and deepest, it is also the coldest body of water in the world, the temperature not rising above 35° Fahrenheit when the summer is at its height. The most skilful and the boldest swimmer may abandon all hope should he have to swim any distance for his life in Lake Superior. The sailor has to exercise the utmost caution when navigating a vessel upon it. Fogs are frequent and they obscure the air in the twinkling of an eye. Without any warning the wind often begins to blow furiously, and lashes the placid bosom of the Lake into tumultuous waves. The Atlantic during a gale is not a grander or a more sublime spectacle, and the navigation of the Atlantic is never a greater test of seamanship than that of Lake Superior when a storm is raging.

Michipicoten Island, distant about a hundred miles from Sault Ste. Marie, is the first regular stopping-place after entering the Lake. The Island rises 800 feet above the water; it is richly wooded, the principal trees being maple, birch, spruce, cedar, balsam and mountain ash. The climate is more temperate than on the mainland. It is probable that the Island may become a favourite place of resort during the summer months on account of the extreme salubrity of the air. The soil, which is a rich vegetable mould mixed with sand, is very well fitted for growing root crops. Beautiful agates are found along the beach. The visitors who busy themselves in searching for agates are generally disappointed, as the keeper of the lighthouse has forestalled them in gathering the finest specimens. Those persons who buy agates instead of trying to pick them up, may amuse themselves profitably by fishing, as speckled trout abound close in shore and can easily be caught.

The Jesuit Fathers who were the earliest explorers of this region of the Continent have left on record many interesting particulars about the mineral riches which abound on the shores of Lake Superior, as well as on the islands in it. Father Dablon, in his Chronicle for 1669-70, thus refers to the Island of Michipicoten: "After entering the Lake the first place met with containing copper is an island

about forty or fifty leagues from the Sault, towards
the North Shore, opposite a place called Missipi-
cooatong (Michipicoten.) The savages relate that
it is a floating island, being sometimes near and
and at others afar off. A long time ago four
savages landed there, having lost their way in a
fog, with which the island is frequently surrounded. It was previous to their acquaintance
with the French, and they knew nothing of the
use of kettles and hatchets. In cooking their
meals, as is usual among the savages, by heating
stones and casting them into a birch-bark pail
containing water, they found that they were
almost all copper. After having completed their
meal, they hastened to re-embark, for they were
afraid of the lynxes and hares, which here grow to
the size of dogs. They took with them copper stones
and plates, but had hardly left the shore before
they heard a loud voice exclaiming in an angry
tone 'who are the thieves that carry off the cradles
and the toys of my children?' They were very
much surprised at the sound, not knowing whence
it came. One said it was the thunder; another
that it was a certain goblin called Missibizi, the
spirit of the waters, like Neptune among the
heathen; another that it came from the Memogoris-
sioois, who are marine men, living constantly under
the water, like the Tritons and Syrens, having long
hair reaching to the waist, and one of the savages
asserted that he had actually seen such a being. At
any rate, this extraordinary voice produced such
fear that one of them died before landing; shortly
after, two others died, and one alone reached home,

who, after having related what had happened, also died. Since that time, the savages have not dared to visit the Island, or even to steer in that direction." Father Dablon concludes by saying that it is commonly believed by the savages that the Island contains an abundance of copper. He also gives a rational explanation of the phenomena which so terrified the savages as to make them shun the spot. The heated stones containing copper which they put into their birch-bark pail may have poisoned the meat and caused the deaths of the eaters; the supernatural voice may have been an echo of their own, while the apparent vanishing and reappearance of the Island may have been due to fleeting fogs.

It is noteworthy that, while the existence of minerals was known to the savages who lived near Lake Superior and was made known by the first European explorers of that Lake and its vicinity, the working of the mineral deposits was not begun there till nearly two centuries later. Stranger still it was ascertained that a race far older than the savages with whom the Jesuit Fathers conversed, a race of which little more is now known than that it existed, must have been extracting copper from the mines at Lake Superior long before Columbus set forth to discover a new world. These people are supposed to be

Mound Builders; in the Mounds which are their only memorials, copper ornaments have been found. The Indians inhabiting the country had no knowledge of mining and no skill in working metals.

In the winter of 1847-8 a most curious discovery was made at the place on the South Shore of the Lake, near the Ontonagan River, where the Minnesota mine is situated. There Mr. Knapp discovered the remains of old workings, and found a mass of native copper, ten feet long, three feet wide, nearly two feet thick, and weighing six tons. The earth has been carefully excavated on all sides, but the metallic mass proved too heavy to be removed. In the vicinity were stone hammers, copper knives and chisels and wooden bowls for baling out water. Had not the copper been deposited here in its native or pure state these ancient people could not have mined it. Yet their operations, though rude, were most ingenious and they were a people which had made a greater step in the direction of civilization than the Indians who succeeded and supplanted them.

While the citizens of the United States have carried on Copper-mining at Lake Superior with great energy and to their pecuniary advantage, the copper deposits of the like nature on the Canadian side have remained almost untouched. The magnitude of the mining operations in this part of the United States may be understood when I add that the amount of metal extracted since their beginning is 300,000 tons in weight and valued at $140,000,000. Several mines have yielded profits which may be literally termed fabulous. The shareholders in the Calumet and Hecla, for instance, receive dividends at the rate of half a million sterling annually on an original capital of forty thousand pounds sterling, the market price of the original capital being about five millions. Indeed, the tales about the yield of the gold mines of California and Australia, of the silver mines on the Comstock lode and at Leadville are not more wonderful than the authentic story of the Copper-mines of Lake Superior.

The purity of the Lake Superior native Copper is remarkable, being as great as that of the same metal found in Japan and in Siberia. The metal is pronounced to be chemically pure, leaving no residuum when dissolved in pure nitric acid, giving no precipitate when the nitric acid solution is heated with ammonia, containing no trace of arsenic or other volatile metal. For electric purposes it is preferred to any other owing to its superior conductivity; hence it commands a higher price in the market and hence, too, the process of mining this native Copper is more remunerative than that of mining the sulphurets of Copper.

When I visited the Island of Michipicoten I learned that its mineral treasures are attracting the attention of capitalists. In addition to deposits of native Copper, resembling those on the South Shore of the Lake, deposits of silver and nickel have been found. With a supineness which it is difficult to understand and scarcely possible to justify, the Canadians allow strangers to reap the profits which the mines in this part of their territory can easily be made to yield. I was told that a company formed in the United States had acquired several acres of land on this Island where they were mining for native Copper and that their preliminary operations had been eminently satisfactory. Still better results were anticipated by the Quebec and Lake Superior Mining Company which had acquired ten square miles of land on the Island. I was unaware at the time of my visit to the Island that the shareholders in that Company were indisposed to furnish the capital wherewith to erect machinery, so as to profit by the explorations which demonstrated that their property was as rich in native Copper as other remunerative properties on the United States side of the Lake. Several months later I returned to England where I learned that a Company called the Michipicoten Native Copper Company had been formed, that Mr. W. W. Stuart, the Chairman of the Quebec and Lake Superior Mining Company, having purchased the majority of the shares, had transferred his interest in ten square miles of the Island of Michipicoten to the English Company for a sum of 50,000*l.* in fully paid up shares, these shares not to rank for dividend till the subscribers of money had received all their capital back out of profits. I was impressed with the stories which I heard on the spot and read about the mineral riches of Michipicoten Island. I was also struck with the unusually favourable terms on which the English Company had acquired a property there, and I thought I should not act foolishly in becoming a shareholder in a Company which not only promised so much, as is the rule in mining companies, but which appeared likely to be one of the companies which supplement promise with performance. Other Companies will doubtless be formed to bring to the surface and divide among shareholders the riches which lie below the surface of Michipicoten. Nor is the mineral wealth confined to the islands in the Lake. The North Shore also is rich in copper and silver; an English company, the Lake Superior Native Copper Company, is now working a property at Maimainse, in Batchewaung Bay, where the Copper in the ore amounts to 69 per cent. while, in addition, the ore contains silver to the value of 36 ounces per ton. Silver Islet was the next place at which the *Frances Smith* stopped. The passage from Michipicoten Island to that spot was made in most disagreeable circumstances. A storm of thunder and lightning raged for five hours ; seldom have I seen so much and such vivid lightning; never have I seen rain fall so heavily ; the water descended in sheets. The storm began at 6 o'clock in the evening; early on the following morning the rain ceased, the wind lulled and the sea gradually went down. A dense fog covered the water. About 8 o'clock in the morning while looking towards the bow, I heard the roar of surf and I saw rocks not far distant on the port side. Captain Robertson, who was on the look-out, at once ordered the engines to be reversed, and the steamer began to go astern in time to prevent any mischief. A delay of a few minutes would have rendered a catastrophe unavoidable. It is improbable that any one would have survived to tell the tale had the vessel first struck upon the rocks and then gone down in the deep, icy cold water. The coolness and rapidity with which Captain Robertson acted were appreciated by the passengers. It was with a tinge of incredulity, however, that they heard him avow he had expected to meet with rocks at the very place where they loomed ominously through the fog.

A few years ago a Montreal Company was seeking for silver on an Islet about a mile from the mainland. Having discovered that the rock was rich in silver the Company sold the property to a few citizens of the United States. These gentlemen have since then taken silver out of this small rock to the value of two million dollars. The Islet is a mass of rich silver ore; it is estimated that eighteen million dollars' worth of silver may yet be extracted from it. The search for silver on other islands, such as Isle Royale, Pie Island, McKellars Island, as well as on the mainland is actively pursued by many persons who have made valuable discoveries. Indeed, the prevailing opinion is that the mineral deposits around Lake Superior and on the islands in it are extensive and rich beyond calculation.

After leaving Silver Islet the steamer enters Thunder Bay, a sheet of water twenty miles in diameter, girded with lofty heights and guarded at its entrance by Thunder Cape, a rugged rocky headland rising 1350 feet above the surface of the Lake. The cliffs of Thunder Cape extend in unbroken surface for a distance of seven miles. When the tempest howls around this mass of rock the echoes reverberate like claps of thunder. The Indians believed the noise to be the voice of the Great Spirit, Nana-bijoo, speaking to them from out of his dwelling in the clouds. The explanation of the tradition is that a volcano at the summit, now extinct, once belched forth fire and lava. A grander or more impressive spectacle than that presented at this spot it is scarcely possible to imagine. Prince Arthur's Landing is a town on the mainland at which the steamer calls, and here the cattle, which had suffered much during the voyage and had caused the passengers no slight discomfort, are sent on shore. The town itself dates from the time that Sir Garnet Wolseley started from this place at the head of the Red River Expedition to suppress Louis Riel's rebellion in Manitoba. Prince Arthur's Landing is a Lake port of the Canadian Pacific Railway, competing with Fort William to the South as the terminus of the line. The town has a thousand inhabitants. It supports two weekly newspapers, one being the *Thunder Bay Sentinel*, the other the *North Shore Miner*. The purpose of the latter is to chronicle the prospects and progress of mining in this region. It contains highly eulogistic articles on the mineral wealth of the Islands in the Lake and of the mainland. The great demand is for capital. Lamentations are indulged in as to the indifference of Canadian capitalists to the development of the riches which are buried underground, and the remark is made that " the

American capitalist is the one on whom we must depend for the development of our rich resources. There are no Canadians who have the push and stamina sufficient for the purpose." A Frenchman, Baron de Guichainville, who has taken up his abode at Prince Arthur's Landing, is labouring to induce his countrymen to invest money in a fish-canning establishment there and also in various mining enterprises. In addition to the deposits of silver and copper which have excited much attention and enriched many persons, this region abounds in vast deposits of iron ore which may prove as remunerative when extracted and smelted as mines of silver or gold.

Not far from Prince Arthur's Landing stands Fort William, an older settlement on the Kaministiquia River where the Hudson Bay Company have long had a trading-post. The rivalry between the inhabitants of the two places is extreme. In each place it seems to be an article of faith that the rival must speedily decay and that the one which remains will increase rapidly in wealth and population. There is ample room and opportunity for both. After a ten hours' sail through scenery of great beauty and variety, the head of Lake Superior is reached and the steamer is moored at the wharf of Duluth, the ambitious city which it was supposed would rival Chicago in quickness of growth, which is one of the best puffed cities on the North American Continent and which is styled by its self-satisfied and grandiloquent inhabitants, "the Zenith City of the Unsalted Seas."

## CHAPTER VII.

#### DULUTH TO WINNIPEG.

Twenty years ago a few enterprising and sanguine men settled on the site of Duluth and resolved to found a city which should excite the astonishment and admiration of mankind. They were also prompted by the desire to eclipse the city at the head of Lake Superior which then seemed destined to become a place of importance. They partially succeeded in their project. It is unquestionable that Duluth has thriven more rapidly than Superior city with which it has maintained a constant rivalry from the outset. Yet the stranger whose expectations are very moderate will be the least disappointed with Duluth. Eleven churches and a few houses scattered upon a hillside are all that meets the eye when the city is approached from the Lake. There is a main street in it containing stores and hotels; there are side streets containing many unoccupied building-sites; there are said to be 5000 people in the city, yet nothing is visible which produces a stronger impression on a new-comer than that made on the least observant stranger by the sight of other pretentious and quite as populous cities in the United States or Canada. It must be apparent, however, to the careful observer that Duluth possesses natural advantages which almost justify the hopes and boasts of its founders. This city is the natural depôt for traffic by way of the Lakes to the interior of the Continent. The opening of new railways to the west has had the effect of increasing that traffic and such increase must continue to benefit Duluth.

Cairo on the Mississippi, the "Eden" where Martin Chuzzlewit nearly lost his life, is commonly supposed to have been more cleverly and justly ridiculed in its younger days than any other city in the United States. Quite as much ridicule has been cast upon Duluth and nothing has served it so well. None of the advantages which this city owes to Nature have helped to make it so attractive as the speech in the United States Congress which Mr. Proctor Knott, a representative of Kentucky, delivered in February, 1871, a speech which was designed to scout its pretensions and to make it the laughing-stock of the country. Whenever the conductors of Duluth newspapers are at loss for something wherewith to fill and enliven their columns, a condition of things which appears to be not infrequent, they reprint Mr. Proctor Knott's speech and, whenever the citizens have nothing better to do, which appears to be a common occurrence also, they re-read it with unconcealed satisfaction. Mr. Knott made for himself a reputation for oratory by this one speech, resembling that which was made in the House of Commons by the member who was not quite accurately nick-named " Single Speech " Hamilton. Mr. Knott's effort is a striking example of that mock heroic vein which is supposed to be the forte of Western orators. It made him and Duluth the subject of general talk and celebrity, if it did not confer upon both lasting fame. It was directed against an application for a grant of land from the national domain which he fancied would advance the growth and foster the prosperity of Duluth. A few extracts will show the character of a speech which produced a more lasting impression than hundreds which have been addressed to Congress in our day and which no sane person would dream of reprinting from the volumes in which they are consigned to oblivion at a large cost to the country. After a laboured introduction Mr. Knott said : " Years ago, when I first heard that there was somewhere in the vast *terra incognita*, somewhere in the bleak regions of the Northwest, a stream of water known to the nomadic inhabitants of the neighbourhood as the river St. Croix, I became satisfied that the construction of a railway from that raging torrent to some point in the civilized world was essential to the happiness and prosperity of the American people, if not absolutely indispensable to the perpetuity of republican institutions on this Continent. I felt instinctively that the boundless resources of that prolific region of sand and pine shrubbery would never be fully developed without a railway constructed and equipped at the expense of the Government, and perhaps not then. . . . Who will have the hardihood to rise in his seat on this floor and assert that, excepting the pine bushes, the entire region would not produce vegetation enough in ten years to fatten a grasshopper? . . . I had been satisfied for years that if there was any portion of the habitable globe absolutely in a suffering condition for want of a railroad, it was the teeming pine barrens of the St. Croix. At what particular point on that noble stream such a road should be commenced I knew was immaterial, and so it seems to have been considered by the draughtsman of this bill. It might be up at the spring, or down at the foot-log, or the watergate or the fish-dam, or anywhere on the bank, no matter where. But in what direction it should run or where it should terminate were always in my mind questions of the most painful perplexity. . . I was utterly at a loss to determine where the terminus of this great and indispensable road should be, until I accidentally overheard some gentleman the other day mention the name of 'Duluth.' Duluth! the word fell upon my ear with peculiar and indescribable charm, like the gentle murmur of a low fountain stealing forth in the midst of roses, or the soft sweet accents of an angel's whisper in the bright joyous dream of sleeping innocence. Duluth! 'Twas the name for which my soul had panted for years, as a hart panteth for the water-brooks. But where was Duluth? Never, in my limited reading, had my vision been gladdened by seeing the celestial word in print. And I felt a profound humiliation in my ignorance that its dulcet syllables had never before ravished my delighted ear. I was certain that the draughtsman of this bill had never heard of it, or it would have been designated as one of the termini of this road. . . . Yet, sir, had it not been for this map kindly furnished me by the Legislature of Minnesota, I might have gone down to my obscure and humble grave in an agony of despair, because I could nowhere find Duluth. . . . The fact is, sir, that Duluth is pre-eminently a central place, for I have been told by gentlemen who have been so reckless of their personal safety as to venture away in those awful regions where Duluth is supposed to be, that it is so exactly in the centre of the visible universe that the sky comes down at precisely the same distance all around it. . . . Then, sir, there is the climate of Duluth, unquestionably the most salubrious and delightful to be found anywhere on the Lord's earth. Now, I have always been under the impression, as I présume other gentlemen have, that in the region around Lake Superior, it was cold enough for at least nine months in a year to freeze the smokestack off a locomotive. But I see it represented on this map that Duluth is situated exactly halfway between the latitudes of Paris and Venice, so that gentlemen who have inhaled the exhilarating airs of the one or basked in the golden sunlight of the other, may see at a glance that Duluth must be a place of untold delights, a terrestrial paradise fanned by the balmy zephyrs of an eternal spring, clothed with gorgeous sheen of ever-blooming flowers and vocal with silver melody of Nature's choicest songsters. . . . Sir, I might stand here for hours and hours, and expatiate upon the gorgeous prospects of Duluth, as depicted on this map. But human life is far too short and the time of this House far too valuable to allow me to linger longer upon the delightful theme. I think every gentleman on this floor is as well satisfied as I am that Duluth is destined to become the commercial metropolis of the Universe, and that this road should be built at once. . . . Nevertheless, sir, it grieves my soul to be compelled to say that I cannot vote for the grant of lands provided for in this bill. . . . These lands, which I am asked to give away, alas, are not mine to bestow! My relation to them is simply that of trustee to an express trust. And shall I ever betray that trust? Never, sir! Rather perish Duluth! Perish the paragon of cities! Rather let the freezing cyclones of the bleak Northwest bury it for ever beneath the eddying sands of the St. Croix." The speech from which the foregoing extracts are taken has been pronounced "the most amusing speech ever made in the American Congress;" it gave its author a reputation which he has not adequately sustained. But the most curious thing is the ignorance of geography shown in it; if a foreigner had made half the number of blunders with which Mr. Knott is chargeable, he would be held up to scorn in hundreds of newspapers throughout the Union, and pronounced a being unworthy to live. If Mr. Knott had spoken about the St. Louis River, his remarks would have had some cogency; if the St. Croix River were to swallow up Duluth it would have to begin by making a journey across Lake Superior. Intending to ban Duluth, Mr. Knott succeeded in blessing it most effectively. The bill which was thrown out, owing to his speech, was opposed by the friends of Duluth, and was supported by the friends of Superior City, of which it was the rival. Indeed, to repeat what I have said and to do so in the grateful words of a Duluth newspaper, Mr. Proctor Knott's speech "gave Duluth the best advertisement she ever had."

For a year before, and for three years after this speech was delivered, the city was in a state of feverish activity. In the spring of 1870, every boat that arrived swarmed with passengers and every stage-coach was over-crowded. A railway was in construction to St. Paul, the capital of the State and Mr. Jay Cooke had projected the Northern Pacific railway which was to run from Lake Superior to Puget Sound on the Pacific. Mr. Jay Cooke suspended payment in 1873 and a panic spread to Duluth from the financial centres of the United States; real property fell to one-fourth of its former price and then, as an eye-witness wrote, "for a few months, there was as much of a *stampede from* Duluth as there had formerly been of a *rush to* the place."

A worse fate than being buried "beneath the eddying sands of the St. Croix River" was reserved for "the Zenith City of the Unsalted Seas." In the days of its prosperity, money had been borrowed and expended in a reckless fashion: when the panic subsided, the citizens who remained behind, found themselves face to face with municipal bankruptcy. Not till 1879 was a compromise effected whereby the creditors agreed to cancel one-fourth of the amount due to them. The most significant sign of the depression then prevailing in Duluth, and the circumstance most deplored by many citizens, was the publication of the newspapers once a week instead of every day. There are two weeklies now, *The Tribune* and *The Lake Superior News.* Should the revival in trade continue, a daily newspaper, that necessary of existence according to western ideas, may again be reissued here. Certainly, the confidence in the city's future which had vanished, has returned in full measure and speculation in land is renewed in the old style. During my visit I learned that pieces of land which could scarcely be sold for $500 six months before were then easily saleable at $1500.

Several sawmills and a blast furnace are in active operation; an industry paying those who take part in it very well is collecting the sand on the shore of the Lake and despatching it to glass-making works, where it is in demand. There is a large elevator for the transhipment of grain and there are well-built docks for the accommodation of shipping. Indeed, Duluth is not only doing a large trade now, but has made full provision for future expansion.

The additional traffic carried over the Northern Pacific Railway when its construction was resumed benefited the trade of this place, while the emigration to Manitoba has had the like effect. The Canadian Government have erected a home for the emigrants who halt here on their way to Manitoba. It is under the intelligent and attentive supervision of Mr. Grahame, the Canadian

Emigration Agent. He told me that the immigrants are often very exacting and are generally very dirty and that those among them who were most stinted in their means and living before they left home, develope the most luxurious tastes after crossing the ocean.

An express train starts once daily from Duluth for Winnipeg. It is not long since the passengers who started for the same destination could not travel farther by rail than Fisher's Landing, on Red Lake River, the average time taken being a week. Now, the journey between the " Zenith City of the Unsalted Seas " and the Capital of Manitoba can be made in twenty-seven hours. The scenery is very beautiful on part of the line skirting the left bank of the river St. Louis. The " Dalles of the St. Louis " are as striking as those of the Columbia River, though on a smaller scale. Within the space of four miles the river descends 400 feet, passing over serrated rocks which are enclosed between high banks, the appearance being that of a series of small and long drawn out cataracts surging downwards.

At Glyndon the passengers for Manitoba change to the St. Paul and Manitoba line, while those for the Northern Pacific continue their journey westwards. There is a second change at St. Vincent, the frontier city between Canada and the United

States, to the Pembina branch of the Canadian Pacific Railway. I have made this trip several times without finding many things worthy of record and I have been quite as unfortunate after having spent a night at Glyndon. Yet emigrants who pass over the line are kept in a state of pleasing excitement from the time they quit Canadian territory till the time they re-enter it. Land agents and speculators are accustomed to travel backwards and forwards in order to persuade the emigrants to make their new homes in the United States. These persons commonly assume the characters of disappointed Englishmen who, having tried Manitoba, left it in disgust, and have found a genuine Eden on United States soil. As the profits of these agents are not small when they manage to sell the land belonging to the Company with which they are connected, they are naturally disposed to make representations of greater strength than trustworthiness in order to effect sales.

I can write from personal experience in this matter. It was erroneously thought by a worthy gentleman that I was on the way to settle in Manitoba and might be induced to settle in Minnesota instead. He told me that many English families were expected to arrive and take up their abodes on the prairie lands of Northern Minnesota and that the representative of an English Company was in negotiation with the St. Paul and Manitoba railway company for 56,000,000 acres. There had been a slight hitch in the negotiations, but my informant added "I guess that will be fixed." He explained that the gentleman desired the Company to let him have the land at $4 an acre and to insert in the deed of sale that the price paid was $8. This gentleman could then make sales in England at a professedly slight advance upon what he had actually paid, while his real profit would be more than double. I was cognizant of a flagrant case in which ignorant persons in England had been made to pay $25 an acre for Minnesota land which could have been bought on the spot for less than $4. I found that the gentleman who was negotiating with the St. Paul and Manitoba Railway for 56,000,000 and who was said to have 170 families waiting to be transported thither from England in the following spring bore the same name as the one who had disposed of land in another part of the country at an enormous profit to himself. I learned also that a second Englishman who was very active in recommending Minnesota as the best place to which his countrymen could emigrate, had been trying to establish a land Company, but had failed owing to insisting not only upon a large commission, but upon a double commission. I do not question the advantage of choosing Minnesota as a place of residence. It may be quite true, as is alleged, that the land in the North-western part of that State is superior to that in the South-west of Manitoba, even though an imaginary line is the only separation between them. The soil may be affected in some occult way by the nationality of the flag flying over it. Yet, after assuming for the sake of argument, the truth of everything that I have heard in favour of this part of the Continent, I still maintain that no folly can be greater than buying land here on the representations of a third party, and that those purchasers of land will have least reason to repent them of their bargains who enter into no contract and make no payment till they have seen the land with their own eyes.

# CHAPTER VIII.

### ON THE RED RIVER OF THE NORTH.

ALTHOUGH the trip to Manitoba by rail through United States territory is generally uninteresting, yet the trip by water is sometimes diversified by incident. The railway attracts all the passengers in winter; but the steamers on the Red River of the North are eagerly patronized during the summer time. Having made the trip all the way by rail and partly by rail and partly by water, I can affirm from experience that, by journeying partly by rail and partly by water, an adequate notion can be formed of the country and its insects, while much more can be learned about the people. Besides, the Red River is a stream of sufficient volume and importance to deserve notice. Compared with the Mississippi, the Red River of the North appears insignificant. Nevertheless, as its length from Elbow Lake, in which it rises, to Lake Winnipeg into which it flows, is 900 miles, it merits a place among the great rivers of the world.

Two Red Rivers are numbered among the notable streams of the North American Continent. One of them rises in the Territory of New Mexico, flows through the States of Texas, Arkansas, and Louisiana, and, joining the Mississippi, helps to swell the volume of the mighty flood which the Father of Waters pours into the Gulf of Mexico. The other, which is known as the Red River of the North, rises in Elbow Lake, in the State of Minnesota. Its source is not far distant from Lake Itaska, which is the fountain-head of the Mississippi. Though that river's course is southward and the course of the Mississippi is northward when both streams first issue from their parent lakes, yet they soon follow the direction which they keep till their race is run. The Red River, in its northerly progress, divides the Territory of Dakota from the State of Minnesota; it enters the Canadian Province of Manitoba at Fort Pembina; it passes by the city of Winnipeg, the capital of that Province, where it is joined by the Assineboine, flowing from the west; it enters Lake Winnipeg, whence it issues under the name of Nelson River; and, finally, it finds its level and a last resting-place in the icy waters of Hudson's Bay. The valley bearing the same name through which it runs is still more remarkable than the Red River itself. For a space which is 400 miles in length by 70 in breadth, that valley is the finest wheat-growing tract on the continent of North America, if not on the habitable globe.

Farming on a scale unparalleled except in California is prosecuted in the Red River Valley. This dates from the year 1875, when several capitalists bought vast tracts of land there. Mr. B. P. Cheney, of Boston, and Mr. Oliver Dalrymple, of St. Paul, purchased 5000 acres of which 3500 were under cultivation in 1879. In 1877 they harvested 42,000 bushels of wheat, 6000 of oats, and 3000 of barley. The machinery on this farm comprises 40 ploughs, 16 seeders, 40 harrows, 16 harvesters, 3 steam thrashing machines, and 3 portable steam-engines. As many as a hundred men are employed at the busiest season. Mr. Cass has a farm of 6000 acres, nearly the whole of which is sown with wheat. Large though these farms are, yet they seem small in comparison with that belonging to Mr. William Dalrymple; it covers 30 square miles. The area sown with wheat in 1878 was 20,900 acres; the yield was 250,000 bushels. Seventy-five reaping and binding machines were used to harvest the crop, the work being done at the rate of 1000 acres a day. This farm is managed on the plan of a factory. It is divided into sections of 2000 acres, over each of which an overseer is placed;

he carries out the orders of Mr. Dalrymple just as a Brigadier-General carries out the orders of the Commander-in-Chief of an army. Comfortable dwellings are provided for the overseers, while there is a boarding-house for the accommodation of the farm-labourers. Each section has its granary, stables, machine-shop, and engine-house. Indeed, the vast estate is really divided into a number of separate farms, each complete in itself, and all subject to a common head. Four hundred and fifty labourers and upwards of three hundred horses and mules are employed on this farm; three bookkeepers are required to register the accounts, and two cashiers to receive and disburse the money. Indeed the whole arrangements are designed to assimilate the production of grain to the operations of a manufactory. The idyllic side of farming has no place here. The farmer is a capitalist; the farm-labourer is called a "hand" and treated as one. Advocates of spade-husbandry will see nothing to admire in this wholesale method of cultivating the soil, and they will maintain that if this system should grow in favour, the day must arrive when, in the United States as in certain European countries, there will be a permanent and rigid separation between the tillers of the soil and its owners. However, while land continues as plentiful and as easily acquired in

North America as it was in Europe during the Middle Ages, when the existing large estates were formed in England, the citizens of the United States will disregard gloomy forebodings and will continue to lavish their admiration upon a successful capitalist like Mr. Dalrymple. His farm is a common topic of glorification among the citizens of the new North-West, and of admiring envy among the dwellers in less fertile parts of the land.

My present purpose is not to linger and describe what may be observed on the Red River within the United States, but to journey along it to the Canadian Province of Manitoba. That river is the silent highway of intercourse between the citizens of the Union and the citizens of the British Empire. A few years ago an Indian canoe was the only kind of boat which traversed its surface. Now steam vessels pass backwards and forwards between St. Vincent, a station of the St. Paul and Manitoba Railway and the capital of Canada's Prairie Province. There has been a settlement of British subjects on this river since the year 1812. Then the Earl of Selkirk, chairman of the Hudson's Bay Company, induced Highlanders, who could not live in comfort on their native heath, to seek a new home in the heart of the North American Continent. Nearly half a century after this settlement was formed,

Dr. Rae, the famous Arctic explorer, informed a Select Committee of the House of Commons that about two months were required to journey from Toronto, in Upper Canada, to the Red River Settlement in Rupert's Land. The Earl of Southesk, who went to hunt in the Hudson's Bay Territory in 1859, saw a steamer on the Red River for the first time. In 1862 the late Lord Milton and Dr. Cheadle experienced on the Red River a painful foretaste of the perils which had to be faced and surmounted before they could begin their toilsome journey across the North-Western Wilderness. Finding that the steamer sailed but once a fortnight, and not caring to wait for it, they started down the rapid stream in a canoe, and endured extraordinary hardships before they reached Fort Garry. Eight years latter Captain Butler was commissioned by Colonel (now Sir Garnet) Wolseley, the chief of the expedition which was sent to suppress Riel's rebellion, to proceed to Winnipeg through the United States. He passed along the Red River in the steamer *International*, and suffered by the way as others have done before and since. The tale of his misery is graphically told in " The Great Lone Land."

The inconvenience of this route caused the Government of Canada to devise another within the limits of the Dominion. This was known as the Dawson route. A traveller over it, who started from Thunder Bay, on Lake Superior, reached Fort Garry in the course of three weeks. The Red River expedition, under Sir Garnet Wolseley, which first passed over this part of the country, took three months to make the same trip. As the Dawson route proved unremunerative to its promoters, it has long ceased to be a regular pathway for traffic and travel between the provinces of Ontario and Manitoba. The traveller who started from the capital of the former province for that of the latter either went to Chicago by rail, thence by another line of railway to St. Paul and Fisher's Landing, where he stepped on board a steamer which carried him to his destination, or else he took the train to the shore of Lake Superior, where he embarked in a steamer for Duluth; thence he proceeded by rail to Fisher's Landing, and by steamer to Winnipeg. But, whichever route was chosen, the time occupied was not less than 11 days, so that Manitoba remained as far apart from the Eastern Provinces of the Dominion as Canada is from England. My first trip to Manitoba was made by rail from St. Paul to Fisher's Landing, thence by water to Winnipeg. Since then the landing-place has been changed to St. Vincent, thus saving the tedious navigation of Red Lake River.

In the spring, when the river is in flood, the 500 miles which separate the two places can be traversed in 48 hours. In the autumn the river is very low and then the passage is very tedious. The return voyage which I made occupied five days and nights. The first part of the journey northwards is easy and pleasant. Leaving the capital of Minnesota by the St. Paul and Manitoba Railway at 5 o'clock in the evening, the passenger reaches Fisher's Landing shortly before noon the following day. Twenty-five miles from the starting-place a stoppage is made at Wayzata, on Lake Minnetonka. This Lake is one of the natural attractions of the State of Minnesota,; it excites even greater admiration than the falls of Minnehaha, which owe much of their popularity to Mr. Longfellow's poetry. The Lake consists of a series of bays, each of which is a lake in miniature, and many are studded with wooded islands. There are 25 of these bays. The Lake is navigable for a length of 17 miles. In olden time it was the favourite haunt of Dakota Indians; they encamped on its margin or on one of its islands. They caught fish in the lake, gathered wild fruits on the islands, hunted deer and other game in the surrounding forests, and procured sugar from the maple trees which beautified the scene. The places of the wild

Indians are now filled with thousands of civilized tourists, who enjoy themselves during the hot months of summer along the shores or on the bosom of the lake. As we proceed northward there is a change in the aspect of the land. The southern part of Minnesota is diversified with wood and rising ground; the northern is genuine prairie, extending to the horizon without anything but a few log houses to vary its flat surface.

The monotony of the night journey was broken by an incident of which I do not desire a repetition. About midnight the car was filled with an acrid and stifling odour; such a smell I had never experienced before. If the pungent and nauseous effect produced by throwing water upon hot cinders were intensified a hundredfold and if all the worst stenches were combined with it, the result would not equal the reality on this occasion. In the morning I learnt that the train had passed over a skunk. The small town, called Fisher's Landing, from which the steamers started was on the model of Western cities. It had two hotels, between which there was nothing to choose, both being as comfortable and attractive as the cabin of an Irish bog-trotter. There were several drinking-saloons and one general store; a sensible notice in the latter was to the effect that persons who came to make purchases were more welcome than those who merely wished to gossip.

Fisher's Landing is on the Red Lake River, a stream which joins the main one at Grand Forks. Steamers plied between it and Winnipeg twice weekly between the months of May and September. The *Manitoba* was the one in which I went, and the *Minnesota* the one in which I returned. They are the property of the Kittson Transportation Company. I gladly acknowledge that the officials of the company and the officers of the steamers did what they could to render the voyage as pleasant as possible. The boats are unlike anything to be seen in England. Their appearance can best be realized by supposing a Thames coal-barge to have a deck and two long furnaces, with boilers above them, placed near the bow, and two steam-engines further aft. The engines work a paddle-wheel which is the breadth of the boat, and revolves at the stern. Above the boilers and engines is a wooden house, containing the saloon and state-rooms. The top of this house forms the upper deck. Pipes conveying steam from the boilers to the engines run under the thin flooring of the state-rooms, which are situated at the sides of the saloon. As the thermometer seldom indicated less than 95 deg. in the shade during this journey on the Red

River, the extra heat from these steam pipes was a superfluity with which the occupants of. the state-rooms could easily dispense.

Though the heat was intolerable almost beyond endurance and far in excess of what most of the passengers had ever experienced, yet it was not the worst infliction. Myriads of hungry and ruthless mosquitoes plied their sanguinary trade in every corner of the steamboat where a human being could be approached. Many black flies rivalled them in assiduous efforts to get food and inflict pain. At a competitive examination a black fly could bear away the prize from a mosquito. He bites with greater force and to a greater depth, and he clings to the surface of the skin with more firmness than a mosquito, while the irritation which he leaves behind lasts longer and is more painful than that produced by his fellow pest. It is a beautiful provision in nature that a real or imaginary remedy is provided for every plague. Everybody knows that there are several "infallible" cures for sea-sickness. Provision of the same kind exists for the protection of the human skin against the bites of venomous insects. A passenger on board the *Manitoba* was the happy possessor of one of these infallible remedies. He had being fishing in Labrador, where the streams are alive with fish and the air is dark with stinging insects, and he had been able to pursue his sport in comfort by smearing himself with a mixture of tar and sweet oil. He was loud in praise of this panacea before the mosquitoes and black flies pounced upon their prey. He prepared himself for the onslaught, and he was kind enough to allow myself and others to do the same by rubbing the skin with the mixture. It was not long before he stated with extreme emphasis that the insects of the Red River must be differently constituted from those of Labrador, because what repelled the latter seemed to attract the former.

The distance from Fisher's Landing to Grand Forks is 12 miles by land. It is about 50 miles by water. The time taken to go between these two places when the water is low varies from 18 to 30 hours. Ten hours were consumed in passing over the worst part, the distance being four miles. I was surprised, not that the steamer made slow progress, but that it made any. The river winds to a degree which is unprecedented. At few parts is the course a straight one for a quarter of a mile in length. What renders the navigation more laborious is that a barge, laden to the water's edge, is generally lashed alongside the steamer; hence the difficulty of rounding sharp curves is materially increased. The stoppages are frequent and tedious. Sometimes they are caused by the barge and the steamer grounding on a shoal, and then a rope has to be sent on shore, fastened round a tree, and dragged in by the steam winch, or "nigger" as it is here called, till the tree is torn up by its roots or the steamer is moved into deep water. At other times long halts are made to repair the stern wheel, the floats of which are often broken by striking against the bank. It is strange, indeed, that the steamer is not seriously injured every voyage. At the narrowest and most curved parts of the river the steamer's bow is forcibly sent against one bank, while its stern is swung round by the force of the current, and each shock shakes it from stem to stern so terribly as to produce the impression that the entire structure must fall to pieces.

When a steamer runs aground or stops for repairs during the day, the cabin-boys, and the crew, who are not on duty, set to work and catch fish. They use long lines weighted with sinkers; a piece of raw meat forms the bait. Cat-fish, gold-eyes, and pike abound in the river, and a good catch of fish is often secured during the interval of waiting. The anglers and the onlookers are kept awake and excited by the insects, which increase in number and energy when the vessel is stationary. · If any one is tempted by the wild grapes or wild plums to go ashore and pluck them, he gladly returns on board. The mosquitoes are even more plentiful and savage on land than on water. On each bank there is a belt of timber; outside this fringe of trees, the prairie stretches its apparently illimitable expanse. The wood, which comprises elder, oak, box, ash, and elm trees, constitutes the supply for fuel and building purposes over a very large area. Rafts formed of the fallen trees are floated down to Winnipeg, where they are broken up and the logs sawn into boards. One of the rafts which we passed was navigated by a woman; a man lay in a rude structure erected upon it. Household furniture was piled up at the sides, the whole being the worldly effects of a couple changing their place of abode. The man, who had kept watch during the night, now slept while his helpmate took her turn in steering.

The steamer stopped at four stations between Fisher's Landing and Fort Garry. The first was Grand Forks, a town in Dakota Territory; the second Fort Pembina, on the frontier between the United States and Canada; the third West Lynn, a Canadian settlement, where is Fort Dufferin, a trading-post of the Hudson Bay Company; and Emerson, on the opposite side of the river, which is one of the rising towns of

Manitoba. A flag showing the letters H.B.C. in white on a red ground was the mark of the Hudson Bay Company being in possession of the fort. An American citizen told me that some of his countrymen were puzzled when they saw this flag for the first time. One of their number thought he had solved the engima of the three letters by saying that they meant "Here before Christ," as, from the appearance of the country, there had not been any change since then.

Sixty miles intervene between the frontier and the capital of the Province. There is very little wood left along this part of the river, the greater part having been cleared away by settlers or by speculators. Farms are to be seen at short intervals; the crops which cover the ground look exceedingly well. The passengers in the steamer experience a change since the stream has run between banks denuded of timber—in other words, the mosquitoes have ceased from troubling. The only insect which skims the surface of the river and which fills the saloon when the lamps are lit is a white-winged one called a "miller." I have seen these insects on the Rhine in the autumn months, but I never saw so many as on this occasion. A constant stream of them is borne along by the breeze; it has the appearance of a bank of snow. The glasses of the steamer's lanterns are covered with these insects; they dash against the glass and then fall down to die among the mass on the deck. They fill pails when the deck is swept in the morning. Though they obscure the light, they give no other annoyance, and they are mere objects of curiosity.

The first I saw of Winnipeg was in the autumn of 1878. Fort Garry, a rectangular building, with a turret at each corner, then stood where the Assiniboine enters the Red River. The steamer stopped a few minutes to land passengers, the permanent landing-place being a short way further down the river. The houses which form the city have a substantial look; the villas on the river's bank are tasteful in appearance. On the opposite side of the river to that on which the capital stands is the parish of St. Boniface, with its cathedral, the palace of Archbishop Taché, its college, and its convent. When Mr. Whittier was here a quarter of a century ago the journey down the river in a canoe seemed to him a wearisome undertaking. He wrote a poem on the "Red River Voyageur," which opens with this vivid and correct description of the river itself:—

> Out and in the river is winding
> The links of its long, red chain
> Through belts of dusky pineland,
> And gusty leagues of plain.

He depicts the "voyageur," when tired and exhausted, regaining his spirits and vigour on hearing the chime of the bells of St. Boniface. Then the poet, as his manner is, ends his verses with a comparison and points a moral :—

> Even so in our mortal journey
>   The bitter north winds blow,
> And thus upon life's Red River
>   Our hearts, as oarsmen, row.
>
> And when the Angel of Shadow
>   Rests his feet on wave and shore,
> And our eyes grow dim with watching
>   And our hearts faint at the oar,
>
> Happy is he who heareth
>   The signal of his release
> In the bells of the Holy City,
>   The chimes of eternal " peace."

# CHAPTER IX.

### THE CITY OF WINNIPEG.

WINNIPEG, the capital of Manitoba, surprised me more at first sight than any one of the countless cities which I have visited on the North American Continent. The older ones frequently surpassed my utmost expectations; the younger as frequently fell below the most moderate estimate which I had formed of them in imagination. Indeed, a pretentious city in the Far West is commonly on a par, in external appearance, with a paltry village elsewhere. I had read much about Winnipeg before visiting it, and the impression left on my mind was not favourable. The Earl of Southesk, who was here in 1859, writes that "there were houses enough to form a sort of scattered town." Lord Milton and Dr. Cheadle, who followed him three years later, saw nothing worthy of note. Captain Butler, who paid it a visit in 1870, refers to it, in his "Great

Lone Land," as "the little village," and "the miserable-looking village of Winnipeg." I knew that changes had been made since Captain Butler came hither on duty connected with the Red River expedition under Colonel (now Sir Garnet) Wolseley; but I was not prepared to find that they had been so great and startling as those which I actually beheld.

Walking down Main-street, on my way to the Pacific Hotel, I could hardly realize that I was in a city incorporated so recently as 1873 and supposed to be far beyond the confines of civilization. The street is 132 ft. wide and it is lined with shops, churches, and public buildings which would do credit to a much older and more famous place. The solid look of the majority of the edifices is as noteworthy as their ornamental design. They are built of cream-coloured brick. It is at a comparatively late stage in the growth of a western city, either in the United States or Canada, that the buildings are composed of anything but wood; hence, a stranger in one of them is apt to arrive at the conclusion that the buildings are erected for a temporary purpose. Here, however, the effect is the reverse. The Town Hall and the Market, the Post Office, the Dominion Land Office, and the Custom House, to name but a few of the public edifices, are as sub-

WINNIPEG IN 1870.

stantial buildings as can be desired. No one looking at them can feel here, as is so commonly felt in other places of rapid growth on this continent, that the citizens apprehend their city will decay as rapidly as it has sprung up. While the progress of Winnipeg is one of the marvels of the Western world, there is good reason for believing that it will continue at an accelerated rate, and that Winnipeg will hereafter hold in the Dominion of Canada a place corresponding with that now held in the United States by Chicago. In 1870 there were 300 people in the miserable-looking village of those days; now, the population is approaching 15,000. There are eight churches—one belonging to the Roman Catholics, three to the Episcopalians, one to the Presbyterians, two to the Wesleyan Methodists, and one to the Baptists. There are several schools and colleges—two common schools, St. John's College Schools, for boys and for girls; a Central School; St. Mary's Academy; Manitoba College, in connexion with the Presbyterian Church, and a Wesleyan Institute. Most remarkable of all, if not altogether exceptional among seminaries for the advancement and diffusion of sound learning, is the University of Manitoba. It grants degrees in arts, sciences, law, and medicine. Its governing body is composed of representatives of religious societies which have not succeeded in working harmoniously for a common end in other parts either of the Old or the New World. The colleges affiliated to it are the Episcopal College of St. John, the Roman Catholic College of St. Boniface, and the Presbyterian College of Manitoba. Others may and are expected to join a University which, if as successful as it deserves to be, will become a model for other places, both on the North American continent and on the continent of Europe. The governing body consists of a Council, composed of a Chancellor and Vice-Chancellor, representatives of each college, three representatives elected by the graduates, and two representatives of the Provincial Board of Education. The first Chancellor chosen to preside over the Council is the Bishop of Rupert's Land, and the Vice-Chancellor is the Hon. J. Royal, the Secretary of State for the Province, and a highly-respected member of the Catholic Church. Provision is made for the colleges affiliated to the University granting theological degrees. No objection can be raised to this by the most advanced and uncompromising educational reformer; indeed, the educational reformer would be hard to please, if he were not satisfied with the constitution and government of the University of Manitoba. While those persons merit unstinted praise who have worked and made no mean sacrifices to render the University successful, the Legislature of the Province is equally worthy to be held in honour for having contributed to aid the experiment by endowing the University. Thus nothing has had to be paid by the colleges which are now in connexion with it, nor will those which may hereafter become affiliated to it have to provide any funds.

Another institution which I did not expect to find in so young a city is the Historical and Scientific Society of Manitoba. Though it has been only two years in existence, this Society has rendered a service to the Province by collecting its records, exploring its Indian mounds and collecting specimens wherewith to illustrate its mineralogy and geology. It is unfortunate that the Society could not persuade the Hudson Bay Company to spare old Fort Garry, instead of levelling it to the ground and using the stones to form the foundation of a new store. However, the Company have wisely presented many volumes of records to the Society's library, where they will be safely kept, and accessible for study. From a personal inspection of the works in the library, and the curiosities in the museum, I can vouch for a good beginning having been made, and I have no doubt that, if the members continue to display the same energy, the Historical Society will prove of infinite advantage to the inhabitants of the Canadian Far West.

The great width of Main-street, which runs north and south, adds to its effect; Portage-avenue, which, like it, is 132 ft. wide, runs west, and is an important thoroughfare; Burrow's-avenue is 99 ft. wide; and the other streets are 66 ft. Indeed, the city is laid out with an eye to its future increase in population. This is specially shown in the care which has been taken to secure open spaces, which will prove of much benefit when the area is more thickly covered with buildings. There are three public parks— Victoria, Burrow's, and Mulligan; the first covers eight acres, the second five, and the third three. There is a race-course and a rifle range. The young men take delight and are very expert in rifle-shooting, their ambition being to obtain a place in the Canadian team which pays a yearly visit to Wimbledon, and there displays a vigorous and fraternal rivalry with the volunteers of the United Kingdom. Several tall chimneys in different parts of the city denote the presence of manufactories. I learn that there are two flour mills, three saw mills, and four planing mills; that there is a carriage factory, a biscuit and confectionery bakery, a distillery; and that there is a brewery five miles distant, where the hops used in combination with malt are the wild hops which abound in the district and can be obtained by any one who chooses to gather them. Hotels of various classes are plentifully provided for the entertainment of strangers, the Pacific Hotel and the Queen's being the two best and largest. The public-houses, or saloons as they are called throughout the West, are many in number; they are under rigid supervision and each is licensed. The licence, which costs $240 annually, is liable to forfeiture in the event of the saloon being badly conducted.

The public markets I found well supplied with butcher's meat, poultry, game, fish, and vegetables. The fish come from the lakes and the rivers, comprising pike, cat-fish, gold eyes and white-fish. I have always thought that none but persons who are nearly starving can really eat pike with any relish. A good imitation pike could be manufactured out of white blotting-paper with small pieces of fine wire interspersed; on being cooked the taste of the fish would be well reproduced by the moist blotting-paper, while the sensation of finding a sharp bone at each mouthful would be perfectly rendered by the stray pieces of wire. One of the fish on the bill of fare at the Pacific Hotel bore the name of Red River salmon. I tasted it and thought it delicious, though not at all like any salmon which I had eaten. It was quite as rich as salmon and had scarcely any bones, resembling a lamprey in this respect more closely than any fish with which I am acquainted. A travelling-companion was quite as much pleased with it as I was. Before eating and praising it, he had warned me against ever eating the cat-fish, which he had seen taken out of the river, and of which he disliked the look as well as the name. He was rather surprised to learn that he had heartily enjoyed and commended cat-fish under the name of Red River salmon.

The vegetables for sale in the market reminded me of stories which I had read at home in the months of autumn. No imaginative writer in a country newspaper ever penned a paragraph about gigantic vegetables that could not be justified by the potatoes, cabbages, and turnips which I saw for sale here, and others which I have seen selected for exhibition. It is a common thing for potatoes to weigh 2 lbs. each and turnips 20 lbs. and for them to be as good as they are heavy. A squash has been produced weighing 138 lbs. and a vegetable marrow 26. Cabbages measuring 4 feet 8 inches and 5 feet 1 inch in circumference have excited the astonishment of other visitors as well as my own, while a cucumber, grown in the open air and measuring 6 feet 3 inches in length, was rightly considered a curiosity. The display of fruit was not equal to that of vegetables, the culture of fruit having been neglected owing to the supply of wild fruit being so varied and abundant. Experiments made in growing apples having proved successful, the gardens here will soon be filled with fruit-bearing trees. Yet it is not wonderful that the early settlers should have been satisfied with what Nature has provided for them, seeing that they had nothing to do but gather and consume an abundance of wild plums, grapes, strawberries, currants, red and black raspberries, cherries, blueberries, whortleberries, marsh and high bush cranberries. If the settlers have not busied themselves about the culture of fruit, they have not neglected the culture of flowers. The little gardens which adorn the fronts of the houses are filled with roses, mignonette, and other flowers dear to English eyes. Never have I seen flowers with more brilliant tints than those of Manitoba, and the brightness of their colours is in keeping with the strength and sweetness of their perfume.

An enumeration of the principal sights in the streets of Winnipeg would be incomplete if I omitted to mention that it contains many stores which for size and variety of the goods kept would do credit to any city, as well as several banking-houses, which have not only a solid look as buildings, but which enjoy the reputation of being sound financial establishments. First there is the Post-office Savings-bank, where depositors receive interest at the rate of 4 per cent., with the advantage of perfect security; secondly, there are branches of the Merchants' Bank of Canada, of the Ontario Bank, and of the Bank of Montreal. In the newest western cities it is customary to find churches and schools, manufactories and markets, shops and banks; but I think no other city than Winnipeg has ever been able to boast of a club-house at so early a stage of its existence. The Manitoba Club was founded in 1874—that is, one year after the incorporation of the city. The club-house in Main-street presents a neat appearance externally, while its internal arrangements are as comfortable as the most fastidious person could expect. Its members number about 80. I can write with the greater confidence in praise of the Manitoba Club, because I had the gratification of being made an honorary member of it and of enjoying its advantages. Though acquainted with many clubs, I know of few wherein dinners are supplied of equal quality at so moderate a charge as in the Manitoba Club. I found that the members enjoyed some articles of food which would be accounted startling novelties in any English club, among them being sturgeon, an excellent fish, and roast bear, a tender and finely flavoured meat. I was more struck with this club than with the fact that Winnipeg possesses two excellent daily newspapers, the *Manitoba Free Press* and the *Daily Times*. A clubhouse is regarded as a luxury in the Far West, whereas a newspaper is held to be a necessary of life. In the town of Selkirk, twenty miles farther north, the few inhabitants decided that they must have a newspaper, and, as there was no printing-press in the town, the difficulty to be overcome was considerable. They agreed among themselves to pay a sum of $500 to the founder of a weekly newspaper in Selkirk, and they advertised this offer, adding that a circulation of 400 copies, at $2 each, was guaranteed for a year. The result was that an enterprising gentleman started from the older part of Canada with a printing-press, and became printer, editor, and newspaper proprietor in Selkirk. The experiment was not successful; the weekly journal lived a year when it ceased to appear and a monthly magazine was issued in the hope that the reading public would give it the support which had been denied to the weekly venture.

Before crossing the Red River and describing

the thriving suburb of St. Boniface, I must devote a few sentences to the Company which was once supreme and which is still a power in Winnipeg. There was a time not very long ago when no person could buy, sell, or reside here without leave from the Governor of Assineboia, the old name for this Province. The Hudson Bay Company had then an actual monopoly of the country and exercised an exclusive jurisdiction over it. It had not been disputed in a court of law that the charter conferred on the Company by Charles II. gave them all the authority to which they laid claim, neither could it be denied that the attempt to keep a fertile region vaster than Europe as the hunting-ground of savages and a breeding-place for wild beasts, was opposed to the spirit of the age. The monopoly ended in 1869, when the Company surrendered its claims to Canada in return for 300,000*l.* in cash, the retention of land round the trading-stations estimated at 50,000 acres, and of one-twentieth part of the remainder of the land. Thus the Hudson Bay Company became the largest possessor of landed property in the world.

In past times no company could well be more prosperous than this one; the proprietors received enormous returns for their investments; the dividends were sometimes as high as 300 per cent.

Not even the East India Company in its palmiest day was a greater financial success than this great fur company of the North-West. And just as the East India Company had among its servants men of genius like Clive and Hastings, so was the Hudson Bay Company served by men whose ability was not inferior to that of the conquerors and rulers of the East. The factors who conducted the Company's trade were proud of their position and did their utmost to uphold it. Once a year they met at Norway-house, reviewed the operations of the previous year, planned those of the following year, and carefully scrutinized each other's performances. The factor who had been weighed in the balance and found wanting was excluded from acting with his colleagues. Indeed, merit was then the indispensable qualification for the advancement of a Hudson Bay Company's servant. In treating the Indians of the North-West, the policy of that Company has been both humane and exemplary. No one, indeed, who has studied the subject and who has had the good fortune to enjoy the acquaintance of the pioneers of civilization in the North-West can refrain from praising the servants of the Hudson Bay Company in the strongest terms. Though that Company is as ably served as of old, yet its exceptional prosperity is a thing of the past. The

P

fur trade must dwindle in importance as the settlers cover the region where the desultory efforts of wild Indians to kill wild animals alone checked their multiplication. The Company must look for its future profits from the sale of land. It is difficult for any body which has certain traditions, and which has prospered by observing them, to forget them altogether and begin an entirely new career, and this is the difficulty with which the Hudson Bay Company have been confronted.

Fort Garry, the original post of the Hudson Bay Company, was at the southern end of Mainstreet. A large store adjoins it, in which all the articles can be purchased which are required either by the simple savage or the exacting white man. Next to the store is the Governor's residence, now occupied by the Lieutenant-Governor of the Province. Formerly this store was the only place where the Red River settlers, for several miles round Fort Garry, could make purchases, or where they could dispose of their produce. Even now the articles sold here are as good and quite as cheap as in the Winnipeg shops; in making this statement, I do so from experience, having been a customer both to the store and to some of the shops. Now, if the Company desired that their store should be able to cope most thoroughly with rival establishments the obvious course was to promote settlement in its vicinity. This was not done; on the contrary, the chief business part of the city was driven northward. Five hundred acres of land at Fort Garry remained the property of the Company at the transfer of its dominion to Canada in 1869. Instead of selling this land to the highest bidder, a price was set on it far in excess of the sum for which land equally good could be bought elsewhere. Hence it is that, instead of the neighbourhood of the Fort and store being covered with dwellings, it lay waste, while dwellings covered the opposite end of Main-street, nearly two miles distant.

A change has taken place in the conduct of the Company's business which is likely to redeem all the errors once committed. Mr. Brydges, who had been Manager of the Grand Trunk and Superintendent of the Intercolonial Railway, was appointed Commissioner for the sale of the Company's land. He has brought his large business-knowledge and tact to bear upon the matter with the best results. There are still changes to be effected in the management of the Company's affairs before they can be said to be conducted in the most efficient manner. Nevertheless, so much has been done in the right direction that the financial success of the Company ought to be far greater in the future than in recent years. About the value of their property there can be no question. To use a phrase common in the United States, "there are millions in it." But prudent management both in London and Winnipeg is required to extract the millions from it.

## II.

It is time, for the sake of variety, to pass across the river to the interesting suburb of this city. A few minutes spent in a ferry-boat, and then the passenger sets foot in St. Boniface. The cha between any part of the English and French c is very great; crossing the Straits of Dover landing in France is like entering a new wc Much the same effect is produced on him leaves Ottawa, passes through the suburb of Edinburgh, crosses the river, and enters Hull. This is not only a change from the Province of Ontario to that of Quebec, but it is also a change from an English to a French speaking locality. Such a contrast may also be perceived, both in the oldest and youngest States in the North American Union. When the river is crossed which separates New York from Hoboken, one passes from an English to a German speaking city; indeed, there are shops in Hoboken where German is under-

WINNIPEG AS IT IS.

stood better than English. In Chicago and Milwaukee there are quarters where German is the prevailing speech, and in St. Paul there are quarters where Norse is the only tongue fluently spoken. But none of these cases is so curious as that of St. Boniface. In the cities of the United States, though the people may speak a foreign tongue, there is yet no external token of the population being foreign. On the western side of the Red River, the wayfarer who looks at the street-corners sees such truly British names as Alfred, Gladstone, and Macfarlane; on the eastern side he sees Rue St. Boniface, Rue St. Joseph, Rue du Moulin, while he hears the passers-by converse in the French language. It is not so much the fact that French is spoken, as that everything looks so French which renders this suburb of the city of Winnipeg unlike any other which I have seen in any city on the continent of North America or of Europe.

The settlement of French half-breeds at St. Boniface dates from the year 1818. Since then it has been the Roman Catholic mission centre of the North-West. Bishop Provencher laboured here as a priest from 1818 till his death as bishop in 1853. His successor, Archbishop Taché, has spent the greater part of a long life as a missionery priest among the Indians. Archbishop Taché's work entitled "Twenty Years of Missions in the North-West of America" is not only an interesting record of personal experience, but till recently it has been the only trustworthy guide to that obscure region. He is very popular, and his great authority over the Half-Breeds and the Indians is exercised with much discretion. He chiefly contributed to allay the irritation which occasioned and succeeded the rebellion headed by Louis Riel; and, though he was said to have rather strained his powers as a mediator by promising an absolution to the rebel leaders which the Canadian Government did not intend to accord, yet he unquestionably acted in good faith and with a success proving that his interpretation of the mission which he undertook was justified by events.

The most conspicuous buildings in the suburb of St. Boniface are connected with the church of which Archbishop Taché is a worthy representative. First in importance is the Cathedral, a stone building in simple Gothic style, and one of the best edifices of the kind in the North-West. Its organ is one of the finest in the country; it was a gift to the Archbishop from his friends in Quebec on the 25th anniversary of his accession to episcopal rank. The interior of the Cathedral is principally remarkable for the absence of the tawdry decorations which so often offend the eye

in such places.  The Archbishop's palace is close
to the Cathedral, and is also built of stone.  It is
a plain, comfortable dwelling-place, with a well-
kept garden in front, filled with flowering plants
and trees.  I had the pleasure of conversing with
the Archbishop and of learning his views with
regard to the settlement of the country.  He has
that polish of manner which seems to be the
inheritance of most persons whose mother-tongue
is French.  Though no longer young and though
much of his life has been passed among hardships
which render a man old before his time, yet he has
the look of a man much younger than his years.
He is a living witness to the salubrity of the
climate, having been here upwards of 30 years;
his predecessor, Bishop Provencher, lived long
enough to show that residence near the Red River
was conducive to longevity.

Archbishop Taché has a strong faith in the
progress of this region of the country and in its
adaptability for settlement.  Some parts further
westward he considers too poor for cultivation,
but he admits there is ample space and attraction
for millions to take up their abodes and prosper.
The task of civilizing the Indians he holds to be
much less difficult than is commonly supposed,
and the success which the missionaries of his
Church have had among the Indian tribes between

the Red River and the Rocky Mountains is strongly in favour of the sanguine views entertained by the Archbishop. His own exertions to promote education are worthy of high praise and have yielded good fruit. Several educational and charitable institutions over which he exercises supervision are within a short distance of his palace. First there is the College of St. Boniface, where the students number between 60 and 70; secondly, there is St. Boniface Academy for the education of girls, where the teachers are Sisters of Charity; thirdly, there is the Convent of St. Boniface, where orphans and destitute old women are cared for and supported by the Sisters; and, fourthly, there is a hospital in connexion with the convent for the relief of the sick. Having read some extracts from the pastoral letter issued by Archbishop Taché at the time of the last general election in Canada, I was desirous of seeing the document itself, and, on stating this, the Archbishop kindly presented a copy to me. I shall translate a few passages from it in order to show the kind of advice which is given to electors by this excellent representative of the Catholic Church in the Canadian West.

He begins by claiming for priests, as citizens, the duty to take part in elections and the right to do so in virtue of their education and sacred office.

He sets forth the importance of the elections on account of the results which may follow, and the necessity of having a well-constituted Legislature. He insists on the value of every vote in a Legislative Assembly, seeing that a single vote may turn the scale for good or evil, and he contends that this consideration ought to be borne in mind in choosing representatives. He controverts the generally prevailing view that any man is fitted to be a legislator, saying that to represent one's fellow-countrymen, to undertake the preservation of the interests of one's country, and to become a legislator are such very difficult and important duties that one is often surprised at the ease with which certain persons set up as candidates and solicit the votes of electors. A proper candidate ought to possess common sense, a thing which the Archbishop holds to be rarer than is commonly supposed, and of which the absence is almost invariably marked by ignorance of the precept there is "a time to keep silence," adding, "Discretion in speech is so charactistic of prudence that we are assured in Solomon's Proverbs that even a fool when he holdeth his peace is counted wise, and he that shutteth his lips is esteemed a man of understanding." He thinks it imperative that a good member of Parliament should be a well-instructed man, "it being possible to be a worthy man without instruction, but not a good legislator." Equally necessary is it to be an honest man, to be received in good society, to be sober and God-fearing in order to merit being sent to Parliament. The Archbishop remarks that these considerations prove that the requisite Parliamentary qualifications are not possessed by all men, and then he goes on to show what are the duties incumbent on electors. The first is to pray for enlightenment, the second to consult wise and discreet persons, to avoid being influenced by passion or personal interest, to widen the sphere of their contemplation, and to consider the public weal. He warns them against the curses of elections, which are lying, drunkenness, venality, and violence, and he implores them to allow the result to be achieved in opposition to their wishes rather than to gain an electoral triumph through perjury, calumny, or falsehood. He denounces bribery as a crime which stains both parties, both the briber and the bribed being bad citizens, traitors to duty and honour. He styles a member who owes his election to corruption as an intruder in Parliament. He charges the electors not to commit any acts of violence and to refrain from copying the bad example in this respect which had been set elsewhere, adding, "Above all show yourselves Christians, and you cannot fail to be good citizens."

He concludes by forbidding the holding of political meetings at the church doors on Sundays and by desiring that such gatherings should be held on weekdays only. The foregoing summary of this pastoral letter not only shows the opinions which the Archbishop inculcates, but it justifies me in asserting that if other dignitaries of his Church displayed the same tact and good taste there would never be any cause for protesting against priestly interference at elections.

Before leaving St. Boniface, I must note that this suburb of Winnipeg promises to thrive even better in the future than it has hitherto done. The terminus of the Pembina branch of the St. Paul and Pacific Railway is here, and this has given an impetus to building. A newspaper in French, called *Le Métis*, is published weekly. It is the only French journal published in the Canadian North-West and taking cognizance of the wishes and wants of the large class there which preserves the use of the French language. There is no part of Canada where speech is more diversified than in the Province of Manitoba, nor is there any in which the ordinary routine of existence is more varied.

# CHAPTER X.

### THE PROVINCE OF MANITOBA.

The surprise which I felt on first walking along the streets of Winnipeg and seeing so many tokens of progress and civilization was increased when I journeyed through the Province of which Winnipeg is the capital. I had read that the country was totally unfit for settlement. I had read that it was pre-eminently adapted for farming and that no other part of the Continent was a more desirable place of abode. Indeed, few regions of the world have been the subjects of greater controversy than Manitoba, the Prairie Province of Canada. It has had many indiscreet eulogists and as many unscrupulous defamers. If the former are right, the Province must be an Earthly Paradise; if the latter set forth the whole truth, it must be the counterpart of Dante's *Inferno*. Though the discussion as to the advantages or drawbacks of this place has been specially keen and persistent of late years, yet the difference of opinion concerning it is of old date. Since the Hudson Bay Company received their charter from Charles the Second in 1670, doubts have been expressed and uncertainty has prevailed as to the character of the region out of which this Province has been carved. The matter was carefully investigated by a Select Committee of the House of Commons in 1749 and again in 1857. Mr. Gladstone was a member of the Committee which sat in 1857 and he was not so ready as some of his colleagues to conclude that the officers of the Hudson Bay Company were justified in maintaining that the entire Canadian North West was unsuited for settlers and had been evidently designed by Providence to be a perpetual breeding-ground of wild beasts and a congenial habitation for wild Indians.

Sir George Simpson, who had been Governor of the Hudson Bay Company's territory during thirty-seven years and who had traversed every part of it, emphatically assured the Committee that the region now known as Manitoba was cursed with a poor soil, a variable and inhospitable climate and disastrous and frequent inundations. The Right Hon. Edward Ellice, speaking on behalf of the governing body of the Company in England, confidently asserted that the Red River district was no place for settlers and that the State of Minnesota, now so prosperous, was no place for them either. Sir John Richardson, the famous Arctic explorer, agreed with the officers of the Company in pronouncing the land utterly worthless for settlement; and he declared that he could not understand why any one should go thither except to prosecute the fur trade. He made a statement which caused an impression on his hearers but which seems very strange to me. It was to the effect that the vine does not grow naturally on the North American Continent to the north of 43 degrees of latitude. Now, I have eaten and plucked grapes on the banks of the Red River to the north of the 49th parallel of latitude, and I have drunk wine made from wild grapes grown on the Assiniboine River at the 50th parallel. When men of experience and eminence like Mr. Ellice and Sir John Richardson made such extraordinary mistakes as to matters of fact relating to this part of the country, it is not to be wondered at if they grievously erred in matters of opinion. In truth, many of the facts and opinions current about Manitoba have been either palpable fictions, or absurd blunders.

The Province of Manitoba occupies the centre of North America, being equidistant from the pole and the equator, the Atlantic and Pacific oceans. Its area when formed into a Province was 14,310 square miles; since then its boundaries have been extended and it now covers 120,000 square miles. In Canada the Provinces of Quebec and British Columbia are the only two covering a larger area than Manitoba, while in the Union two States only, Texas and California, are vaster than it. Yet Manitoba covers but a fraction of the Canadian Far West, there being ample space therein out of which to carve fifteen other Provinces of the like extent. Its peculiarity and advantage consist in the fact that settlement there is of an old enough date to enable its capacity for producing food and affording pleasant homes to the landless to have been thoroughly tested. When I visited it in 1878 for the first time the novelty of the scene fell short of my expectation. I had been accustomed, in common with many other persons, to regard it not only as outlandish and inaccessible, but as a region where life must be spent under even less favourable conditions than in those remote parts of the Far West with which I was acquainted. With a feeling of amazement, then, I discovered throughout Manitoba innumerable indications of a long-settled and well-governed country. Many of the farms which I visited had an antiquated look which produced a striking impression. I had expected them to resemble other Prairie farms, which appear as if they had just been established, or were on the point of being abandoned, everything about them being unsubstantial and unfinished. The rude dwelling-houses seem intended to serve a temporary purpose. No trim gardens give evidence of long residence and the expenditure of leisure time. An unenclosed plot of ground, in which cabbages or potatoes are struggling for existence among a mass of weeds, is the only attempt at gardening to be seen on a new prairie farm. The fields bear testimony to the haste with which the settler has striven to grow and garner a crop. He has sown the seed before the land has been wholly reclaimed from its wilderness state, caring nothing about appearances so long as he can harvest a quantity of grain sufficient to repay his outlay and to leave him a surplus wherewith to feed himself and his family. Tidiness is not the forte of a prairie farmer.

In Manitoba, however, many prairie farms have as finished and comfortable a look as any in Great Britain. An enclosed garden, filled with flowers and vegetables and free from weeds, is attached to most of them; the fields are in excellent condition; the dwelling-house seems built to last and to afford a comfortable shelter; an air prevails which can best be rendered by the epithet home-like. This was not what I had come so far to see. Yet, if I had pondered more carefully the history of the country, it is precisely what I ought to have expected. It is a common but an entire mistake to regard Manitoba as a region of the globe in which farming is an experiment. The truth is that farming has been practised there on a considerable scale and with remarkable success since the year 1812.

At the beginning of this century the problem of how to deal with the poorer Highlanders caused much anxiety to philanthropists and statesmen. The semi-patriarchal state in which the Highland clans had lived was a thing of the past, and there appeared to be no place for the members of these clans in the new state of things. Shortly after the bloody suppression of the rebellion of 1745, many Highlanders emigrated to North America. Expatriated Highlanders constituted the bone and marrow of the colony which General Oglethorpe conducted across the Atlantic in order to found what is now the State of Georgia. Others had chosen North Carolina as their dwelling-place, and, siding with Congress in the war of Independence, they proved themselves sturdy and dauntless soldiers in battle.

In the introduction to Scott's *Legend of Montrose* an account is given of Sergeant More M'Alpin who, having served his time in the army and been discharged with a pension, went back to his birthplace in the North of Scotland and found that a single farmer occupied the ground where two hundred persons had lived in his boyhood. He meditated following them to Canada and settling in the valley which they had called after their native glen. Lord Selkirk persuaded some of these evicted Highlanders to unite in founding a colony on the banks of the Red River of the North. He had become Chairman of the Hudson Bay Company and he had acquired a tract of land covering 116,000 square miles, whereon he wished to form a settlement. In the spring of 1811, a party of Highlanders, the majority being natives of Sutherlandshire, embarked at Stornaway and sailed for York Factory on Hudson Bay. It was autumn before the party reached York Factory, and the land journey to Fort Garry, on the Red River, could not be begun till the following spring; the emigrants did not reach their destination till the autumn of 1812. The weary and dispirited Highlanders found that they were expected to fight as well as to farm, hostilities being then in progress between the Hudson Bay Company and the North-West

Fur Company of Canada and they were told that, if the latter Company were victorious, they would be deprived of the land which they had bought. So hard did their lot seem that they resolved to quit the country, and they had actually started in 1816 when, on Lord Selkirk appearing with a fresh band of emigrants, they agreed to remain. Their descendants in the third generation are now successful and prosperous farmers, and it was their farms which struck me as very different from the Prairie farms which I had seen elsewhere. Their experience demonstrates how fertile the soil is along the Red River Valley.

I visited farms in the parish of Kildonan where wheat had been sown and where crops had been reaped for sixty years in succession without manure being applied. Indeed, the Red River farmers have long regarded the natural fertilizers of the soil as an incumbrance of which they try to rid themselves with the least possible trouble. Their habit was either to cast manure into the river or else to build out-houses in such a way that it might fall down and be no more seen. When this region passed from under the jurisdiction of the Hudson Bay Company and became a Province of Canada, one of the earliest legislative enactments provided that the farmer who polluted a river with manure should pay a fine of $25, or else be imprisoned for two months. Even now it is more common to collect the manure in heaps than to strew it over the land. The only fertilizer added to many fields is the ash from burned straw. I often saw the straw, remaining after the grain had been thrashed, set on fire as the quickest way to dispose of it. However, as the country becomes more thickly peopled, straw will be taken to market and sold for money instead of being converted into ashes.

That a piece of land should bear wheat for three generations in succession is extraordinary, but that the yield at the end of that period should amount to 25 bushels an acre is more extraordinary still. On virgin soil the yield is enormous. The best evidence on this head, because it is perfectly authentic, is that furnished by Mr. Senator Sutherland, a native of the Province, to a Committee of the Dominion House of Commons in 1876. Mr. Sutherland then said that he had "raised 60 bushels of spring wheat per acre, weighing 66 lbs. per bushel, the land having been measured and the grain weighed carefully. I have also received reliable information to the effect that 70 bushels of wheat have been produced from 1 bushel of wheat sown." Another interesting fact rests on the same trustworthy authority; this is the abundance of grass and cheapness of hay. The prairie grasses, of which there are six varieties in this Province, contain much nutriment; they can be converted into hay at the cost of $1 a ton. These wild grasses often grow to the height of 5 feet; the yield of hay is as much as 4 tons an acre.

While the descendants of the original settlers are living in comfort, the new-comers are prospering also. They have to struggle against certain drawbacks as is the lot of all prairie farmers; in their case, however, it is emphatically true that patience and perseverance have their reward. I conversed with many of the later settlers. One of them was a very intelligent man who had emigrated from the North of Ireland to Ontario fifteen years ago and who had migrated to Manitoba a year before I saw him, being induced to do so because the return from his farm did not keep pace with the increase and the demands of his family. His flock of a dozen children gave him no concern in his Manitoba home. His eldest daughter had found a good place at a liberal wage in a clergyman's household, while his crops were so abundant that he could easily feed all the mouths dependent upon him and lay something aside for the future.

He had but one fault to find with the country, and he was not singular in his complaint. The violence of the thunderstorms appalled him. I was not surprised to hear him say this. I have had some experience of thunderstorms and I am prepared to maintain that those of Manitoba are so terrific as to be beyond all rivalry. In Ontario the flashes of lightning are more vivid and the peals of thunder are far more resonant than in England, but a Manitoba thunderstorm is to one in Ontario what one in Ontario is to one in England. When Manitoba is visited with such a storm the rain falls as if the windows of heaven were open, the thunder crashes as if the celestial combat imagined by Milton were at its height, the lightning fills the air with sheets of dazzling brightness athwart which dart tongues of flame. The air is so charged with electricity that the simplest operation reveals its presence. It can be made manifest by merely combing one's hair. At times it appears in a startling fashion. The Earl of Southesk records in the narrative of his travels here that, when about to wrap himself in a fur robe, "a white sheet of electrical flame blazed into his face, for a moment illuminating the whole tent."

The Manitoba farmer who reaps fabulously large crops can afford to bear the discomforts of occasional thunderstorms of exceptional violence. When locusts, or grasshoppers as they are here called, visit the country they cause greater uneasiness because they occasion far greater loss than all the thunderstorms. This plague is not peculiar to Manitoba; it is dreaded by farmers in the Western States from Minnesota to Colorado. At Denver, the capital of Colorado, I once saw a flight of grasshoppers, resembling a scintillating brown cloud, pass over the city, and many were the speculations among the onlookers as to the part of the State on which it would descend and work destruction. The settlers in Manitoba have suffered less from this pest than their neighbours in the United States. Since the first settlers came here in 1812 the grasshoppers have appeared thirteen times, whereas they have visited the State of Minnesota six times since 1855; in the former case the visitations having been thirteen during sixty-eight years and in the latter, six during twenty-five years. The Indians welcome grasshoppers; they catch, roast and eat them and pronounce them very good. Happily for the farmers, who prefer bushels of grain upon which they can live, to bushels of grasshoppers which devour their crops, the voracious insects are not regular visitors. As many as thirty-five years have elapsed between their successive appearances. Moreover, the farmers are better able now to ward off their ravages than they were in bygone days.

Grasshoppers are an infliction which is not very frequent nor very greatly feared; the spring floods are annual torments for which no remedy has yet been adopted. They cause the farmer much annoyance and serious loss. The deposit left upon the land which has been inundated frequently lessens its fertility for a season. There is a remedy which would cure all this, or better still which would prevent the mischief altogether. A lightning-rod guards the farmer's house and barns from injury by the electric fluid. A proper and general system of drainage would shield his fields from the destroying flood when the snow melts in the spring and the streams are swollen to a great height. The Government of the Province have a comprehensive scheme of drainage in contemplation. If it were carried out and if it proved effectual, the wealth of the Province would be vastly augmented, the waste now produced by the floods being incalculable.

The Red River cart is a relic of Manitoba in the old time which is destined to follow the buffalo and be seen no more. Indeed, it cannot outlast the buffalo, because buffalo hide is one of the chief materials used in its construction. The cart is entirely made of wood and buffalo hide, no metal being employed or required in its construction. It was an ingenious device of the first settlers who, having no iron at their disposal, had

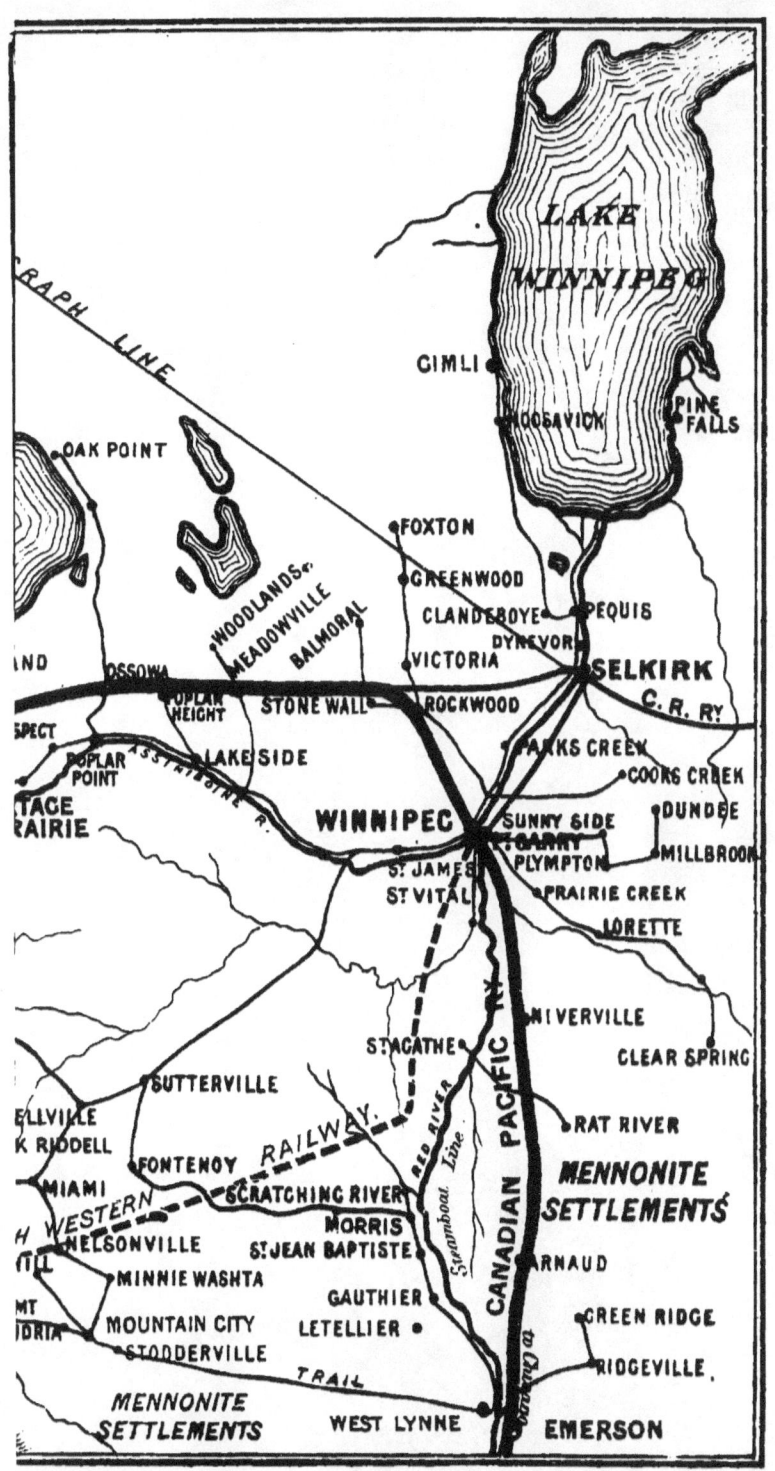

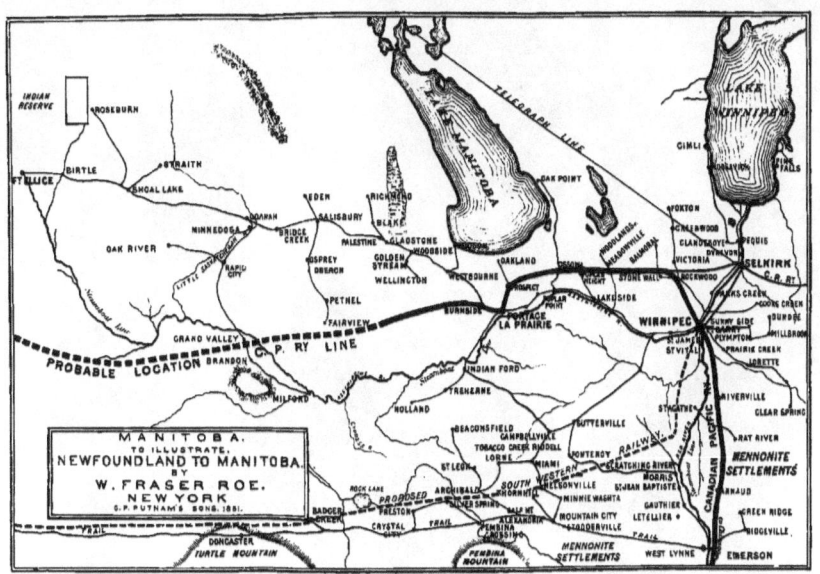

to contrive to dispense with it. Such a cart costs $10; it is light as well as cheap, and a heavier load can be drawn in it by an ox over the soft prairie than in a cart of another build. With one of these carts carrying a load of half a ton, a yoke of oxen, a plough and a few other implements, the Manitoba farmer is equipped for tilling the soil. Farming on the prairie is very different work from farming in the backwoods of Canada. It has been aptly and truly said, "Where the Ontario farmer ends, the farmer of Manitoba begins." The latter has merely to plough the prairie, sow the seed and wait till his grain is ready to be reaped; he has neither trees to fell nor land to clear.

Any citizen of the British Empire can get a farm in Manitoba on very easy terms. The Canadian Homestead Act provides that he may secure 160 acres of land on paying an office fee of $10, living there three years, erecting a dwelling on it not less than 18 feet long by 16 feet wide, and cultivating a part of the land. On complying with these conditions, he becomes the absolute owner of the land. His task is not hard. He may grow a crop the first year of occupation which will reimburse him for all his outlay. Should he have cattle, they can graze free of cost on the prairie grass and be fed in winter on hay hich he obtains for the trouble of cutting and curing it. In order to succeed he must start with capital; the minimum sum which he ought to have on beginning to farm is $500; the larger his capital the greater his chance of success. In any case he must make up his mind to endure some privations, to eat very plain food, to sleep little and work very hard. Should he be diligent in toiling with his hands, he may count upon being in comfortable circumstances at the end of five years and a rich man at the end of ten. The fault will be his own if he fail. Nature has done everything for the Manitoba farmer that nature can do for any farmer, and it rests with him to do the rest. The Manitoba farmers whom I visited and with whom I conversed are so conscious of this as to indulge but seldom in the grumbling which is the failing of the farming class. I found them more ready to express thankfulness than to find fault. It was their rule to use nearly the same form of words in which to convey their reply to my question as to what they thought about the country as a whole, the phrase being "Manitoba is the finest land that God's sun ever shone on."[1]

[1] Among the many pamphlets, Blue Books and works relating to Manitoba which I have read, none contains a more interesting and valuable account of its early history than a book entitled *Red River*, by Mr. J. J. Hargrave, published at Montreal in 1871.

# CHAPTER XI.

### MENNONITES AND ICELANDERS IN MANITOBA.

The emigration of the Mennonites from their Russian homes near the Sea of Azoff to new ones near the Red River of the North, is an interesting fact in contemporary history. These Mennonites are German Protestants who reject infant baptism, who will not bear arms or take an oath. Their ancestors took refuge in Russia a century ago because they were not allowed to practise their religion in Western Prussia. They found an asylum in Russia where the edicts of successive Emperors allowed them to till the soil and live in peace. It was decreed, however, that the immunity which they had enjoyed from military service should terminate in 1871; hence, they had either to submit to the conscription or leave the country. The majority chose the latter alternative.

A large number of Mennonites emigrated to the United States, settling in Nebraska and Kansas.

A small body went to Brazil, suffered much and returned to Russia after undergoing great privations and after being the objects of English charity during their stay at Southampton, on returning from Brazil, and till permission to reenter Russia was granted. While the exodus was in progress, Mr. Hespeler was commissioned by the Canadian Government to proceed to Russia and suggest to the Mennonites that Manitoba would be a suitable place for them. A few Mennonites had settled in Ontario, had prospered, had grown rich and were disposed to succour their unfortunate brethren in the dominions of the Czar. They agreed to become sureties to the Government of Canada for the repayment of any sum which it might be necessary to advance to the Russian Mennonites by way of loan. The amount lent by the Government was $80,000, at 6 per cent. interest, repayable in eight years.

Before deciding to leave Russia for Canada, the Mennonites sent three agents to survey the land and empowered them, if satisfied with it, to select a tract for settlement. These agents reported very favourably of Manitoba, and they chose two places one to the East, the other to the West of the Red River, as suitable for their brethren. The Canadians were not impressed with the penetration of these agents, because the land which they deliberately selected seemed far inferior to other land which they might have had. When the main body of the Mennonites arrived at the Red River about five years ago, they had much to endure. They had to encamp on the open prairie in the cold winter months. Water was scarce and trees were few in number. They dug wells and met the first difficulty; they built houses of sun-dried brick and overcame the second and, what was still more wonderful, they heated their dwellings and cooked their food with fires made without wood or coal. I mentioned in a previous chapter that the early settlers had a habit, which they bequeathed to their descendants and from which the latter are not yet weaned, of burning the straw in their fields and casting their manure into the river. The Mennonites carefully save both. They thatch their houses and barns with part of the straw; the remainder they mix with the manure, press the two together and cut the mass into cakes, which serve admirably as fuel to burn in their clay-built stoves. These stoves are so arranged that three sides of each form parts of three rooms, thus distributing heat over the greatest surface and economizing fuel.

More cosy dwellings and better arranged farm offices than those of the Mennonites are not to be found in Manitoba or in the Canadian Far West.

The furniture is plain but substantial, and well adapted for its purpose. It is the handiwork of the people themselves. They employ their leisure in carpentry during the frost-bound winter months. The men think it as absurd not to make their own chairs and tables, their writing-desks and chests of drawers, as the women consider it inexcusable not to suckle their infants and make the clothes used by their families. It is the custom of both sexes to buy anything which they can fabricate for themselves. They are thoroughly practical Christians; they hold that their duties to themselves and their neighbours consist in dressing plainly, being diligent in business and rendering to every one his due and no more. They are ready to help those who help themselves; but they will not lend a hand to keep the idle by nature in a state of blissful indolence. The men are farmers from choice. No drones are suffered to remain in their community. Every one in sound health is obliged to labour with his hands or to pay the penalty of starving. A clergyman toils in the fields during the week and ministers to the spiritual wants of his flock on Sundays. Nor is the schoolmaster exempted from manual labour during seed-time and harvest; the rest of the year he is permitted to teach the children. The women have to labour as hard and as unremittingly as the men. No distinction of sex is made when a field has to be weeded, a house plastered, seed sown or cattle tended. All who can use their hands are obliged to do so when the occasion arises.

The Mennonites will not fight on any provocation. They will not take an oath whatever the consequences. They will not go to law if they can possibly help it, and they carry their independence to such an extreme that each one acts as his own physician without thinking that he is chargeable with folly. They can the more easily dispense with drugs and doctors because they enjoy exceptionally good health. The country and the climate suit them. I was told by those whom I questioned on the subject that, in Manitoba, they had far less sickness, especially among the children, than in Southern Russia. They are temperate; but they are not water drinkers on principle. They relish a glass of whiskey and still more a glass of brandy if they can enjoy it without payment. Their chief objection to strong liquors consists in having to pay for them. They also delight in a pipe, if tobacco be supplied to them gratis.

I spent a night in one of their settlements; I visited many of their farms; I conversed with several of them in their own tongue. It is a proof of their innate and intense conservatism that they have preserved their German speech till now. It is doubtful whether they will not be driven to speak English as well as German and, in time, to speak English exclusively. In Russia they had no temptation or inducement to learn the language of the country. They were a comparatively educated body placed among an ignorant and, in their estimation, an inferior race. If the Russians by whom they were surrounded wished to converse with them, they held it to be the business of the Russians to acquire their language. Now the tables are turned. They find it necessary to learn English in order to do business with their neighbours, these neighbours not caring to take any trouble for the purpose of being able to converse with them. Whereas in Russia they looked down with contempt upon their ignorant neighbours, in Manitoba they recognize that their neighbours are better educated and far more advanced in the ways of the world than themselves. The agricultural implements which they saw in Canada were as much superior to those which they had used in Russia as a railway train is to a stage coach. They felt that the people who made and employed such improved ploughs, thrashing machines and harvesters must be infinitely their superiors. They showed their tact and good sense, not only in recognizing this, but also in buying the novel implements of agriculture wherewith to cultivate the soil.

Their satisfaction with the soil and climate is expressed without reserve and in the strongest terms. Each of those to whom I addressed a question on this head informed me that the soil of Manitoba was more fertile, that the yield of grain was larger, that the quality of the grain was better there than in Southern Russia, while the climate, especially in summer, was far superior. Some of them waxed enthusiastic when speaking of their Canadian home. They have nothing to complain of. The Canadian Government have pledged themselves to respect the religious scruples of the Mennonites. The Mennonites, on the other hand, desire nothing so much as to be left in the undisturbed enjoyment of what they style "a beautiful, a heavenly land." Their feelings are manifested in the names given to their villages, these being "Schönthal," "Blumenort," "Schönwiese," "Rosenthal," signifying Beautiful Valley, Flowery Spot, Beautiful Meadow, Rose Valley.

Though the Mennonites possess many virtues and make excellent settlers in a new country, they are yet far from being model citizens. Their very virtues are not easily distinguishable from vices. They are as avaricious and niggardly as

French peasant proprietors. They are morbidly suspicious of persons who do not belong to their body and, when dealing with strangers, they drive bargains which are so hard as to verge on sharp practices. To get money is their chief aim in life, and their whole enjoyment consists in labouring for that object. Like other assiduous cultivators of the soil, they allow their minds to lie fallow. They can read and write ; indeed, they would be ashamed of being unable to do both ; but they consider it no reproach to be indifferent to literature other than school-books, hymn-books and the Bible, and never to look at a newspaper. They are utterly heedless as to the affairs of the world, so long as they can reap their crops and make a profit by selling their produce. If they learn what is the market price of what they have to sell, they have learnt all the current information which they care to possess.

Even the charity of the Mennonites has its dark side. The poorer brethren are assisted by the richer, but the richer take care lest the poorer should be so well paid as to grow independent and make their own terms. Rich Mennonites are thoroughly convinced of the advantage of employing cheap labour. Their astuteness as a community is sometimes carried far beyond permissible limits. I was present when the heads of one of their Municipalities were taken to task for the following conduct. In common with others in the Province, this Municipality had received $400 from the Provincial Government to be applied in drainage. The grant was accepted by the Municipality in question, but nothing was done in draining the land. Unless each Municipality did its duty, the effect of the work would be impaired. The result of investigation was to show that the Mennonite Municipality had expended $75 in buying two drainage ploughs which were carefully stored away, and had lent the rest of the sum at interest to a member of their own body.

It is the desire and hope of the Mennonites in Manitoba to live apart from their neighbours and to preserve their own speech and customs as they did in Russia. There are many places on the North American Continent where colonies have been established which have preserved most of the characteristics of their founders. In Nova Scotia and Ontario there are German settlements; in New Brunswick there is a Danish settlement; in Ontario there is a Highland settlement; in many parts of the country there are French settlements. But these settlements are chiefly characterized by two languages being spoken by the people; those among them whose ancestral tongue is German, Gaelic or French learn English also and the fact of the people speaking two languages is the chief, if not the only distinction between them and other Canadians. Every year the possibility of remaining a class apart is more difficult owing to the increase of intercommunication. The present generation of Mennonites may practise all the exclusive rules to which they have been accustomed and their ignorance of English will render it easier for them to resist any external influence which might cause them to modify or alter their views and habits. Their children will assuredly succumb to these influences. They are learning English and they will acquire ideas which must alter their mode of life. Moreover, the Mennonites are making money more rapidly than they ever did before and the sons of rich parents may cease to labour with their hands as their forefathers have done for generations. It is to be hoped, however, that they will preserve some of their simple tastes and all their domestic virtues. The Mennonites have taught the Canadians many lessons, and they have learned much in return. The progress of their community deserves to be watched with interest. As tillers of the soil they have no superiors. As pioneers in subjugation of the wilderness they cannot be rivalled. Their gospel of labour is sound and profitable doctrine for settlers in the Far West, and it is their merit to practise it with diligence and zeal. As Lord Dufferin remarked in an admirable speech delivered when visiting their reservation, they are useful recruits and comrades in a contest waged with Nature where no blood is shed or misery wrought. Yet the war " is one of ambition, for we intend to annex territory, but neither blazing villages nor devastated fields will mark our ruthless track; our battalion will march across the illimitable plains which stretch before us as sunshine steals athwart the ocean; the rolling prairie will blossom in our wake, and corn and peace and plenty will spring where we have trod."

## II.

Fifty-six miles northward of Winnipeg is Gimli, the Capital of New Iceland. The territory set apart for the Icelanders covers 27,000 acres; the population did not much exceed 1029 at the close of 1879; about 500 Icelanders of both sexes were scattered over the Province, the men working on farms, the women as domestic servants. Lord Dufferin was an enthusiastic advocate of immigration into Canada from Iceland. He had learned from personal observation how hard life was in Iceland itself, the people there existing as he phrased it " amid the snows and ashes of an arctic volcano." The first Icelandic settlement in Canada was made in 1875 near Burnt River in Victoria County, Ontario. The spot reminded the Icelanders of their native land far too well, the chief product of the locality being rock. It was then resolved to offer them a tract of land in the Far West on the shore of Lake Winnipeg, provided that they would remove thither and induce their countrymen to join them. The removal was effected the following year and as many as 2000 took up their abode near Lake Winnipeg, an inland sea as long as England and not less abundantly stocked with fish than the salt ocean around Iceland. Immediately after arriving, small-pox broke out among them and they were subjected to a species of quarantine; they complained of being kept too strictly isolated and that intercourse with the rest of the world was forbidden them long after all risk of contagion had ceased.

Perhaps no settlers in the Far West have had more difficulties to surmount than these Icelanders; certainly, none have found anything so strange and unlike what they had seen before. As Lord Dufferin justly remarked, the business of the Canadian settlers is to fell wood, plough fields, make roads; these Icelanders, however, had never seen in their native isle, a tree, a cornfield or a road, and they were ignorant of the very elements of agriculture. It is highly creditable to them that they have learned very quickly how to cultivate the soil, the neat gardens round their comfortable houses being pleasing tokens of their progress. They have been successful in rearing cattle and they have now added beef to their dietary; formerly they lived entirely on fish, vegetables and bread. I am not sanguine, however, about the hopes of the promoters of the settlement being realized. Immigration from Iceland does not continue. For a time the desire of the Icelanders to persuade their brethren at home to join them was so marked that Mr. Lowe, Secretary to the Department of Agriculture, informed a Committee of the Dominion House of Commons, "almost every settler in New Iceland appears to be an immigration agent." The great changes which these Icelanders have undergone appears to have created in their minds a longing for further change and fresh wandering. Some of them have proceeded to the United States and those who remain are not satisfied with their lot. They are a good-tempered and harmless race, they make excellent servants, but they appear lacking in the qualities which constitute successful colonists.

# CHAPTER XII.

### THE NORTH-WEST TERRITORIES.

"Go west, young man, and grow up with the country," was the pithy, sensible and often-quoted advice which Horace Greeley gave to such of his countrymen as were unable to get suitable employment in the Eastern States of the Union. The result has been to people the Western States with men who find it easier to grow rich there than in the place of their birth. What the younger citizens of the United States have been doing for many years back, the young Canadians are doing now. They, too, have a Far West which is as rich in golden opportunities as that which used to be regarded as the most favoured part of the North American Continent. Large and important though Manitoba undoubtedly is, there is a region beyond it still larger and still more attractive. Many persons fancy that Manitoba is far enough west, yet others regard it as on the threshold of the new and marvellous country for which they are bound, and they treat it as a mere halting-place in their journey towards the setting sun.

When the Canadian Pacific Railway is finished and open for traffic the journey westward through Manitoba will be an easy one. At present it is tedious and trying. During a part of the year there is communication by water between Winnipeg and Portage la Prairie, 70 miles to the west, and it is also possible to go in a steamer as far as Battleford, the Capital of the North-West. But the more general mode of travel, and the one which will be followed till the railway can be used is for travellers thither to start in a light spring waggon, carrying a tent and other encumbrances in view of the probable necessity of having to camp out. The traveller and the emigrant do not require long experience of Manitoba to thoroughly understand its greatest drawback, the absence of good roads. The word road has seldom a place in the language of the people, the common expression to designate the pathway between two places being "trail." It may be said, indeed, that each traveller makes his own road. If he be aware of the direction which he ought to follow, he chooses the part of the prairie where the ground is best fitted for driving. Nothing is easier than to drive over the stoneless and springing turf of the virgin prairie and, if the traffic be not too great, an excellent "trail" is made by the passage of successive vehicles. But, when the traffic is heavy and continuous and holes are formed in which water settles and the soft mould resembles a mass of tenacious mud, then following the "trail" is a weariness to the flesh of man and beast. The roads of Manitoba must have much in common with the famous roads in the Highlands before the advent of General Wade.

When England was supposed to be the land of mirth and song, the persons who regard those bygone days with regret would feel themselves disenchanted if they were suddenly transplanted to the gold age of their dreams. English roads were then in much the same state as those in Manitoba now. The Slough of Despond through which Bunyan makes Christian struggle at the beginning of his heavenward pilgrimage to the Celestial City, was doubtless copied from something which he had seen near Bedford. No clearer or more accurate representation of a Manitoba "slew" has ever been furnished than that which Bunyan wrote by way of illustrating the obstacles which Christian had to face and surmount at the outset of his journey. Christian had but one to cross, whereas the pilgrims bound for the Canadian North-West have to cross hundreds. The stoutest-hearted emigrant who has resolved to settle on the Saskatchewan River and who has begun what he considers the last stage of his journey at the Capital of Manitoba, has felt his courage and confidence fail him long before he has reached the first town of importance. Between Winnipeg and Portage la Prairie the mudholes are so many and so difficult to cross that, if they had intercepted Christian's path, he would inevitably have returned in despair to the City of Destruction. Many emigrants have seen them and turned back in dismay. Some explorers of the land have done likewise. One of the latter warned me against making an attempt which must end in failure, if not in the fracture of my neck. It is simply impossible to depict the difficulties caused by those "mudholes;" as difficult is it to persuade the new comer that the "mud" which he regards with horror and disgust is the finest alluvial soil which can be found anywhere. It is no uncommon occurrence for a train of freight waggons, bound westward, to be detained several days in the "mudholes" which intersect the beaten path a few miles to the west of Winnipeg. The emigrants who have surmounted these obstacles to their progress and who remain confident of ultimate success are the persons who not only deserve success but reap it.

An emigrant who has made up his mind to seek a new home in Manitoba can easily prepare himself, before leaving home, for what he must encounter on the way to his homestead in the Canadian Far West. Let him practise crossing a newly-ploughed field for hours together with a horse and cart and pitching a tent at the end of his journey. Let him arrange so that there are frequent ponds in the field, these ponds being at least five hundred yards in width, having an average depth of four feet and a muddy bottom. If he be not disheartened by exercise of this kind he is well qualified for starting on a trip to the Canadian Far West during the wet season. He may be agreeably surprised at other seasons by finding the roads in a very different condition. In the autumn they are sometimes as dry and hard and smooth as a road paved with asphalte. During the winter months they are always good, for then the hard frozen snow covers the prairie and any vehicle in the form of a sledge skims over it as easily as a train runs along a line of rails.

The emigrant or traveller who is prepared to camp out will find life on the prairie far less unbearable than if he depend for shelter at night in a settler's hut. It is trying to toil along the miry paths over which thirty miles are all that can be conveniently passed between sunrise and sunset, but the accommodation at the few stopping-places on the beaten track is quite as great a trial to the fastidious wayfarers. These prairie hotels are the rude log-houses erected by settlers who add to their incomes by entertaining travellers. They are commonly 18 feet long by 16 feet wide and are divided horizontally into two parts. On the ground floor is the place where the family and the visitors sit and take the meals which are cooked in a stove at the one end, the stove serving the double purpose of heating the house and affording the requisite facilities for cooking. In the upper story the occupants of the house pass the night. The food is plain and simple enough to satisfy the greatest foe to high living, consisting of fried salt pork, bread, potatoes and tea. Eggs and milk are luxuries rarely obtainable. Why the settlers do not rear poultry or keep cows is a question which I cannot answer. A few of them add to their incomes, not only by entertaining the strangers who present themselves, but also by levying a toll upon their vehicles. If a stream near their dwellings be difficult to ford, or if the " trail " be in good condition over their land, they construct a rude bridge across the stream and make the persons who use it or who pass over their land pay 25 cents each. I found that some of these astute men put as much as $50 weekly into their pockets by so acting. The emigrants curse these imposts, but they have either to pay them or submit to serious inconvenience. The Government ought to see that the roads are kept in better order and that they are free to all who pass over them. I was told that the Provincial Government are awakening to their duty in this respect. If they give effect to their praiseworthy intentions, many a settler who has to travel over the prairie to his homestead, and to whom every dollar is precious, will grumble less about a matter which ought never to have formed one of his troubles.

When I left Winnipeg for the Far West, the first place at which I halted for the night was Whitehorse Plains where Mr. House combines farming with innkeeping. He has been twenty years in the country and he likes it very much. He regrets the good old days when game was plentiful, life was easy, when the settlers were few in number and hunters were in the majority. The road between Winnipeg and Portage la Prairie, the first place of any importance on the Western road and about 70 miles distant from the Capital, is worse than in any other part of the country I have visited. The population of Portage is 1200. It is the most westerly place visited by Mr. Pell and Mr. Reade, the representatives of the Royal Commission on Agriculture, during their scamper through Manitoba. I found that these gentlemen had made a deep impression upon those with whom they came into contact. It was admitted that, if they saw but little of the country, they were assiduous in rigorously questioning everybody they met. Both gentlemen expressed themselves greatly struck with what they saw and both admitted that Manitoba was a wonderful land. Mr. Reade embodied his feelings as a British farmer in terms which were certainly emphatic. Being asked what he thought of the country, he replied that he regarded it in the same light that a lamb does the butcher. It is impossible to view the vast expanse of land covered with crops of wheat and of a still larger area of as good land still uncultivated without arriving at the conclusion that the Manitoba farmers, who pay no rent, are dangerous rivals to British farmers who both pay rent and obtain a far smaller return for their labour. The average yield of wheat here is thirty-five bushels an acre. If the land were farmed with as much care as is the rule in Great Britain, the yield could be nearly doubled.

The Hudson Bay Company have a store at the western division of Portage, under the care of

Mr. Gigot. I found him a well-informed and most courteous gentleman of German origin. I learned from him that the supply of furs has not yet fallen off. He told me that some wild animals are more plentiful now than before the arrival of so many settlers; he explained this by saying that these animals have always been more numerous in particular years and that the last two years are remarkable in this respect. Moreover, the hunters use more effectual weapons for killing them than in bygone days, so that the return is necessarily larger. It is obvious, however, that the fur-bearing animals which still abound here must disappear before the advance of civilization.

I shall not mention in detail all the places at which I halted during the ten days that I journeyed through the North-West Territory. The farthest point I reached was Rapid City which, by the devious route I followed, is 200 miles to the west of Winnipeg. The weather was very bad during a part of the time and those persons who have traversed the prairie in an open waggon when snow or rain is falling will not wonder that I curtailed my journey. I could not, then, visit the young and aspiring city of Gladstone in the township of Palestine, of which I saw a plan representing it to possess many fine buildings and parks, but which, like other young prairie cities, doubtless looks most attractive on paper. Not far fro it is the township of Beaconsfield which is less advanced than Gladstone city. In Beaconsfield there are only a few shanties and a post-office, whereas Gladstone has a population large enough to support a weekly journal, the *Gladstone News*.

Rapid City is situated on the Little Saskatchewan River and seems destined to grow in size and importance, being the centre of a splendid agricultural district. It was two years old at the time of my visit. I counted 54 houses and a saw mill, and I was told that the population numbered 400. A weekly journal the *Rapid City Enterprise*, after a life of six months, had just ceased to appear and the citizens were occupied in devising measures for supplying a successor to it. A young Canadian journalist arrived at the same time as myself, his purpose being to make an arrangement with the citizens. It was agreed that he should receive a bonus of $500, an office rent free and a lot of land in a good situation, in the event of his publishing a journal for twelve months. The citizens were well pleased with the success of the Show of the Rapid City Agricultural Society, the first which had been held and one which they were glad to think was far better than the first held in the City of Winnipeg. A thousand visitors came to see the sight and the articles exhibited were highly creditable They comprised all those commonly seen at Agricultural Exhibitions and some which would not be found at such an Exhibition in England. The latter consisted of articles manufactured in the locality and of needlework, prizes being offered for the best set of horse-shoes and the best pair of gentleman's or lady's boots, for the best panel door and window sash and the best pair of woollen socks and mitts, for the best rug or mat and the best sack of flour. All varieties of needlework, from plain sewing to the most elaborate embroidery, figured in the prize list. I thought it perfectly sensible to encourage local skill in all the cases where it can be turned to profitable account. When the railway is open the articles which have now to be made on the spot, will be made by machinery, and though brought from a distance, will be sold at a lower price than handmade goods produced at home. It does credit to the managers of the Show that they offered a special prize to the Indians for the best display of agricultural products.

The land in the vicinity of Rapid City is rolling prairie interspersed with small lakes; the soil is lighter than that of Manitoba, yet it is not less productive. Three miles to the South-West is "the English Reserve," a tract of land covering 12 miles square and chiefly occupied by immigrants from England. I visited some of the farms and I conversed with many of the settlers. Several had emigrated with too little capital, others had done so under the delusion that a knowledge of farming was not essential, and both those who had too little money and too little practical knowledge had found their task very severe. But I heard no other complaint than one to the effect that the country was too thinly peopled. All the practical farmers had done well, having reaped large crops and obtained good prices for their produce. The wheat was pronounced by an expert who accompanied me to be the finest he had ever seen. An Ontario farmer, who had been here a year only, was enchanted with the country. His seed sown in a shallow furrow on the wild prairie had yielded a vast increase. The root crops surprised him most of all, potatoes grown on the prairie sod averaging 2 lbs. in weight and turnips from 15 to 20 lbs. each. Some of the farms were very charming. One of 320 acres, obtained at the cost of 33*l*. by a Herefordshire farmer who had left England owing to the failure of his crops in 1879, was everything that any one could desire. A small lake lay in front of the house; a few trees grew close at hand, about twenty acres had been sown with wheat, a smaller portion had been devoted to root crops. A small patch before the door had been sown with flower seeds brought by his daughter from the old home, and the sight of the flowers was as delightful to my eye as the large yields of grain and vegetables. More luxuriant mignonette I never saw before; the flowers were gigantic and the delicious perfume was not impaired by the size of the plants. I was so struck with these flowers as to carry away specimens, being convinced that they were as curious as any specimens of agricultural products and quite as striking testimonies to the goodness of the soil and climate. If the settler in Manitoba be not contented, he has but to migrate to the North-West Territories in order to find a still better farming country. There is plenty of room for all comers in these Territories; they cover more than two and a half million square miles. A low estimate of the finest land available for settlement shows that there is ample room here for a population three times larger than that of the British Isles.

The Hon. David Laird, Governor of the North-West Territories, was on a tour of inspection during my visit, and I had the gratification of much personal intercourse with him. He is a native of Prince Edward Island; he admits that the fertile soil and pleasant climate of his island home are quite matched by those of the great country over which he is now placed in authority. He even thinks that Battleford, the capital of these Territories, is healthier than that of any other part of Canada. Though the attention of the world has been concentrated on this region owing to its reputed value for grain producing, yet, in Governor Laird's opinion, the region is even better adapted for rearing cattle. He described a tract of country not far from the base of the Rocky Mountains which has long been the home of the buffalo, and which is unrivalled for stock rearing; it is 360 miles long by 100 broad; it is covered with rich grasses, and the climate is so temperate that cattle can remain all the winter in the open air with impunity. Underneath the soil, throughout the whole of this tract, there are beds of lignite of the best quality, the lignite burning nearly as well as ordinary coal.

I was pleased to learn that the Indians are giving no further trouble than to make appeals for food when the season is unusually inclement. Some of these Indians are setting an excellent example to their brethren. When Governor Laird went to Battleford in 1877 he found a body of Crees, numbering 600, encamped there. He persuaded them to leave a place where they had no right to remain, and to settle on a spot to the south which belonged to them. The Rev. Mr. Clark, a Church of England missionary, was labouring among these Crees. He had gained their confidence, and he induced them to begin cultivating the soil. He showed them how to set to work, and in 1878 they had good crops of potatoes. In 1879 they had crops of various sorts of vegetables and of some kinds of grain sufficient to provide for their wants, and leave them a surplus to sell. Other Indians are copying what the Crees have done, and it is probable that the experiment so successfully begun on a small scale will prove of inestimable benefit to the Indians as a body. They must cultivate the soil, be fed by the Government or starve. Year after year buffalo are growing scarcer. Once the Indians become habituated to tilling the soil, they will give even less trouble than they now do to the Canadian Government.

Out of consideration for the Indians and in continuance of the policy of the Hudson Bay Company, the sale and manufacture of intoxicants are absolutely prohibited throughout the North-West Territories. The Governor-General of the Dominion is alone empowered to give a licence for manufacturing intoxicants there, while the

Lieutenant-Governor of the Territories may issue a licence allowing them to be sold or kept, under the condition of making an annual return to the Minister of the Interior of the licences issued and of the quantity and nature of the intoxicants to which they refer, that return to be laid before Parliament. Owing to attempts to defeat the operation of such an Act the definition of intoxicants is made to include every conceivable form of intoxicating beverage or solid substance, the words of the Act being: "The expression 'intoxicating liquor' shall mean and include all spirits, strong waters, spirituous liquors, wines, fermented or compounded liquors or intoxicating fluids; and the expression 'intoxicant' shall include opium or any preparation thereof, and any other intoxicating drug or substance, and tobacco or tea mixed, compounded or impregnated with opium, or with any other intoxicating drug, spirit or substance, and whether the same or any of them be liquid or solid." Though not himself a total abstainer on principle, the Governor has become one during his term of office on the ground that he could not well enforce the Act if he made himself an exception to its provisions. He is beset with applications for licences; indeed, the enforcement of the law against the use of intoxicants gives him more annoyance and labour than any other of his duties. He thinks the prohibitive system works well on the whole. Whether it can be upheld when the country is more densely populated remains to be seen. The newly-arrived settlers complain bitterly about the Act. An English farmer's wife told me that she missed her glass of beer at dinner more than anything else, and that if she could enjoy it again, she would not regret having left her old home.

At present, the Governing body of the North-West Territories is nominated by the Governor-General in Council; provision is made, however, for the nominated being transformed into an elected body. Whenever any district of 1000 square miles contains a population of not less than 1000 adults, exclusive of aliens or unenfranchized Indians, the Lieutenant-Governor may proclaim it an Electoral District and desire the people to return a representative. Should the number of adults rise to 2000 then a second representative may be returned. When the Council shall consist of 21 elected members then it shall cease to be a Council and will become the Legislative Assembly of the North-West Territories. This transformation is now in progress and, when it is completed, it will be seen whether the people desire to continue the prohibitions as to intoxicants which are now imposed upon them by the Dominion Parliament.

# CHAPTER XIII.

### THE CANADIAN FAR WEST.

It is a misfortune that the most widely-read descriptions of the vast and sparsely peopled region of Canada, extending from Lake Superior to the Rocky Mountains, chiefly relate to its appearance in the winter season. Hence the notion prevails that the "Great Lone Land" is an illimitable wilderness, covered with snow and intersected with frozen rivers over which people journey on sledges drawn by unruly dogs. All countries in the temperate zone have their winter, yet it produces a misleading impression to depict them as if the winter state were the normal one. I have seen snow lying thickly in sunny Provence and in the Riviera along the Mediterranean which is supposed to be an Earthly Paradise, and I have felt the cold more keenly there than I have done when Fahrenheit's thermometer indicated 20° below zero in the coldest part of the North

American Continent. A lesson soon learnt, and not rapidly forgotten by the visitor to the part of North America where the winters are most severe, is that the position of mercury in a thermometer is no criterion of the cold experienced. So long as the air is still, any person warmly clad is almost insensible to cold. When the temperature is at the lowest point in Manitoba, it is the rule for the air to be absolutely still. At Pau, in the Pyrenees, the thermometer frequently falls far lower in winter than at Nice on the Mediterranean; but, as the atmosphere is so calm at Pau that, for days or weeks together, not a breath of wind stirs the withered leaves on the trees, the sensation of cold is much less than in the warmer but more agitated air of Nice. During a Canadian winter, the sky is clear and the sun shines brightly day after day, and hence, though the mercury may be very low and the indicated cold very great, the feeling is one not of depression but of exhilaration, and the fact of the cold seems to be forgotten. Admiral Sir George Back told a Select Committee of the House of Commons in 1857, that at Fort Reliance, near the Arctic Ocean, he had seen Fahrenheit's thermometer indicate 70° below zero. Being asked as to the effect of the extreme cold on himself and his party, he replied, "I cannot say that our health was affected differently to what it would be in any other extreme cold; perhaps the appetite was considerably increased."

Professor H. Y. Hind, being questioned on the subject of climate by a Committee of the Dominion House of Commons in 1878, said, "The winter cold of Manitoba is greater than the winter cold on the coast of Labrador. But it is a dry uniform cold, and it is very far less inconvenient to the senses, or in any other way, than the moist cold of Labrador." Professor Bryce of the University of Manitoba, gives the following corroborative testimony: "The winters of the North-West, upon the whole, are agreeable and singularly steady. The mocassin is dry and comfortable throughout, and no thaw, strictly speaking, takes place till spring, no matter how mild the weather may be. The snow, though shallow, wears well, and differs greatly from eastern snow. Its flake is dry and hard, and its gritty consistence resembles white slippery sand more than anything else. Generally speaking, the further west the shallower the snow, and the rule obtains even into the heart of the Rocky Mountains. In south-eastern Ontario the winter is milder, no doubt, than at Red River; but the soil of the North-West beats the soil of Ontario out of comparison; and after all, who would care to exchange the crisp, sparkling, exhilarating winter of Manitoba for the rawness of Essex in South Ontario?"

A common mistake is to assume that what applies to one part of the Canadian Far West is true of the whole. No man can speak of the whole from personal knowledge. A great part has not even been explored. The extent of this territory is so vast that the mind cannot form a clear conception of it from statistics. To say that its area is 2,764,340 square miles is merely to set forth large figures. A clearer and more striking idea of the enormous expanse may be formed when I add that it is seven hundred thousand square miles larger than the German Empire, France, Spain, Italy and Russia in Europe put together. These countries support a population exceeding 186,000,000. In the Canadian Far West, the population, including Indians, is probably under 200,000. It is not thought an extravagant estimate to put the future population of this territory, when it shall have been rendered easily accessible, and when its advantages have exercised their full effect in attracting settlers, at nearly 100,000,000. Sanguine observers maintain that the country can support a population of twice that amount.

A territory so vast is exposed to varied natural conditions. The fauna and flora differ in different places; the soil is not everywhere the same, and the climate is as diverse as the soil.

Every hundred miles to the west of Winnipeg there is an increase in the temperature and, when the part is reached where the warm wind from the Pacific—the Chinook as it is called locally—makes its influence felt, the change in the climate is very marked.  There the snowfall is light. Indeed, at the summit of the Yellow Head pass through the Rocky Mountains, snow melts as it falls.  In the grazing-ground at the eastern base of these mountains cattle remain out all winter, finding their own food.  Everything necessary for the sustenance of man is provided in this region.  Farming or cattle-rearing is not the only industry by which wealth may be acquired.  There is ample scope for the miner and even for the manufacturer.  Beds of lignite and ironstone extend over hundreds of miles, so that a little enterprise is alone wanted for the establishment of iron foundries and factories of all kinds at the base of the Rocky Mountains.

I cannot too often repeat that farmers act unwisely in going to the fertile West, unless they can get their produce conveyed to market at a low price.  If the price of grain be very low at New York or Liverpool, the farmer who is at the furthest point from either place is at the greatest disadvantage.  The price which he obtains for his grain is lessened by the cost of carrying it to market, while his own outlay in growing it will be as great as that of a farmer who is within easy reach of the place of sale. It is certain that, if the Canadian Far West be peopled in proportion to its capacity, and if the population grow wheat to the extent that is possible, then the conveyance of this surplus to market will be the most important problem to solve. Farmers have found in the United States that, by settling too far West, the cost of transport eats up all the profit which they would make by growing grain if the market were nearer at hand.

The Canadian Far West cannot be fully peopled until it is more accessible to immigrants; hence it is that the Canadian Pacific Railway is imperatively necessary. Upon that railway the agricultural population must chiefly depend for transporting their produce to market. There is room and there will be employment for a second trunk line two hundred miles to the north of the one now in course of construction. An independent line, the South Western, is to run three hundred miles west of Winnipeg, between the boundary-line and the Canadian Pacific, opening up the rich country in what is called the Turtle Mountain district.

I have journeyed over several hundred miles of the Canadian Pacific between Winnipeg and

Thunder Bay and I was impressed with the advantage of the line for developing local, as well as for accommodating through traffic. This part of the country has attracted less notice of late than the Western prairie land. It is a region of lakes and wood, interspersed with tracts of fertile soil where crops could be grown, and expanses of meadow whereon cattle could be reared. In several parts mineral discoveries of importance have been made. I saw specimens of gold quartz taken from an island in one of the lakes. I was told that an abundance of quartz equally rich had been found; if it be true that quantities of quartz rich in visible gold are obtainable, then gold mining will become a most remunerative industry here. This, added to its other advantages, will lead to the peopling of the region between Lake Superior and Winnipeg quite as rapidly as that of the agricultural region farther west. It may be that the prophecy made by Sir George Simpson in 1841, after he had been twenty years Governor of the Hudson Bay territory, may be speedily fulfilled, a prophecy which, it is fair to add, he stated in 1857 was made in a fit of enthusiasm. Writing about Rainy River which connects the Lake of that name with the Lake of the Woods, Sir George stated:—"From Port Frances downwards, a stretch of nearly one hundred miles, it is not interrupted by a single impediment, while yet the current is not strong enough materially to retard an ascending traveller. Nor are the banks less favourable to agriculture than the waters themselves to navigation, resembling, in some measure, those of the Thames near Richmond. From the very brink of the river, there rises a gentle slope of greensward, crowned in many places with a plentiful growth of birch, poplar, beech, elm and oak. Is it too much for the eye of philanthropy to discern, through the vista of futurity, this noble stream, connecting, as it does, the fertile shores of two spacious lakes, with crowded steamboats on its bosom, and populous towns on its borders?"

The impression made upon me when I passed over nearly a hundred miles of the line to the West of Winnipeg was that there, too, local traffic would be developed. The total length of line required to connect the present Canadian railways with the Pacific ocean is 2627 miles. The struggle over the choice of routes, and over the way in which to carry out the undertaking, has been protracted and severe. A Syndicate has been entrusted with the execution of the gigantic work. The conditions under which the Syndicate enters upon its labours were thus set forth in the Dominion Parliament by Sir Charles Tupper, Minister of Railways: "For that portion of the line from Fort William to Selkirk, 410 miles, the Pembina branch, 85 miles, and that portion from Kamloops to Burrard Inlet, 217 miles—all of which, amounting to 712 miles when the line is completed, is to be handed over as the property of the Company. The total amount expended and to be expended by the Government, including everything, is 28 million dollars. For the construction of the road from Lake Nipissing to Fort William, 650 miles, and from Selkirk to Kamloops, 1350 miles—2000 miles in all—the Government have agreed to pay, in addition to the 28 millions, 25 million dollars and 25 million acres of land; making a total subsidy, in cash, of 53 millions, and in land estimating the 25 million acres at the same rate that I have estimated the land under the contract of 1873, and under the estimate of the Act of 1874, one dollar an acre, of 25 million dollars, or a total amount to be expended by Canada for the construction of the Canadian Pacific Railway of 78 million dollars."

While the Canadian Pacific Railway will shorten the journey between Liverpool and Yokohama or Hong Kong, and while it will both link together the Provinces of the Dominion and aid in developing their resources, it will not entirely solve the problem of transporting agricultural produce at the cheapest rate from the Canadian Far West to Europe. In the United States the route by way of the Mississippi has an enormous advantage over any other; wheat can be carried from St. Paul, the capital of Minnesota, down the Mississippi in barges to New Orleans, where it is transferred to steamers bound for Glasgow, at 38 cents a bushel. It ought to be possible to sell this wheat on arriving at its destination at a lower price than the prevailing one. With the great river as a silent and easy highway, the farmers in the Mississippi Valley can successfully compete with farmers in other parts of the Union.

In the important matter of water-carriage the farmer in the Canadian Far West has unrivalled advantages. The navigable rivers cover a distance of 11,000 miles, of which 4000 only have as yet been turned to account. The distance from Winnipeg to the mouth of the St. Lawrence is 2500 miles, and the transit of bulky articles over this intervening space would be costly. But, if instead of choosing the route of the St. Lawrence as the outlet to the Atlantic, the route by Hudson Bay be chosen, then Winnipeg may be brought within two days' journey by rail and water from the sea.

For two centuries the Hudson Bay Company sent their stores into what is now the Canadian Far West, and took their furs out of it in sailing ships which plied between England and the Bay. The Nelson River connects Lake Winnipeg with

Hudson Bay; it is a vast stream, draining an area of 360,000 square miles, and is six miles wide at its mouth. There are impediments to the continuous navigation of the river by large vessels, but these have not hindered canoes being used for the purpose. It is proposed, however, to make a railway over the 370 miles which intervene between the lower part of Lake Winnipeg and the mouth of the Nelson River. Grain could be stored at Port Nelson and conveyed to England in steamers during the season of navigation. Professor Hind considers "the head of tide-water in Nelson River may yet become the seat of the Archangel of Central British America, and the great and ancient Russian northern port—at one time the sole outlet of that vast empire—find its parallel in Hudson Bay." The water-route by Nelson or Hayes River from Hudson Bay to the interior has proved available for the purposes of trade since the incorporation of the Company in 1670. In 1846 the route was used to convey troops and found suitable. A force consisting of a wing of the 6th Foot, a detachment of Artillery and a detachment of Royal Engineers, with one 9-pounder and three 6-pounders and numbering 18 officers, 329 men, 17 women and 19 children, made the journey by boat from Hudson Bay to Red River in about 30 days. Colonel Crofton, who was in command, made the journey in seven days' less time. The current being strong, it takes far longer to make the journey up stream; including stoppages it has been made down stream, in loaded boats, within nine days. If steam launches were substituted for the boats propelled by hand, the time would be decreased. But it is proposed to dispense with the river altogether, and to make a narrow gauge railway from the northern end of Lake Winnipeg to Hudson Bay and a charter has been granted for such a railway. There is a difference of opinion whether Fort Churchill may not be a preferable port to Port Nelson. But there is agreement as to the feasibility of reopening communication between England and the Canadian Far West by way of Hudson Bay.

It is true that the navigation of Hudson Bay is only open for steamers during five months in each year, yet, during that time, it would be easy to export all the produce which may be destined for the markets of Europe, and to import all the goods which might be required in exchange. The distance from Port Nelson to Liverpool is nearly a hundred miles less than from New York. It is estimated that when steamers shall ply between Hudson Bay and the Mersey, the Clyde or the Thames, it will be possible to sell Manitoba wheat in the United Kingdom at 28s. a quarter and to do so at as large a profit as that now obtained from the sale of United States wheat at 48s. Should that day arrive the British farmer must renounce growing wheat; he can barely hold his own now with his rival in the United States; he cannot possibly compete hereafter with his brother in Manitoba. It may then be found that the desperate struggle in progress between farmers in this country and their competitors across the Atlantic will arise between the farmers on the opposite sides of the boundary-line in North America. The Manitoba farmer will hereafter be able to defy rivalry in the markets of Europe.

No question is more fiercely debated than the relative advantages of different parts of the North American Continent. If a stranger to the country listened to the evidence adduced in favour of a particular State in the Union, or a particular Province of Canada to the exclusion of any other State or Province, he would think that a conclusive case had been made out. Should he listen to the statements made about all of them, he will be either completely puzzled or remarkably acute in sifting and weighing facts. Instead of giving my own conclusion concerning the Canadian Far West as a place for settlers, I shall cite the conclusion of a thoroughly competent and impartial investigator, who has long studied the matter on the spot and who is justly regarded as an authority. This is Mr. J. W. Taylor, the United States Consul at Winnipeg, who has served his country there since 1870. Like all his countrymen, he is a firm believer in the great destiny reserved for the United States, yet his patriotism has not blinded him to the attractions and resources of the part of the Canadian Dominion wherein he resides.

Mr. Taylor's opinion, enunciated in many speeches and writings, is that the North American Continent is divisible into three zones, the southern being the Cotton-growing zone, the mid-zone being specially adapted for the growth of Indian corn, and the northern for the production of wheat. He holds that the mid-zone extends to Southern Minnesota: he stated in a public speech "that three-fourths of the wheat-producing belt would be north of the International boundary." In a letter to the *Pioneer Press* of Saint Paul, he gave the following reasons, among others, upon which he based his conclusion: " In 1871, Mr. Archibald, the well-known proprietor of the Dundas Mills, in Southern Minnesota, visited Manitoba. He remarked that the spring wheat in his vicinity was deteriorating—softening, and he sought a change of seed, to restore its flinty texture. He timed his visit to Winnipeg with the harvest and found the quality of grain he desired, but the yield astonished him. 'Look,' said he, with a head of wheat in his hand; 'we have had an excellent harvest in Minnesota, but I never saw more than two well-formed grains in each group or cluster, forming a row, but here the rule is three grains in each cluster. That's the difference between twenty and thirty bushels per acre.' More recently, Professor Maccoun, the botanist of the Pacific Railway Survey, has shown me two heads of wheat, one from Prince Albert, a settlement near the forks of the Saskatchewan, latitude 53 degrees, longitude 106 degrees, and another from Fort Vermillion, on Peace River, latitude 59 degrees, longitude 116 degrees, and from each cluster of the two I separated five well-formed grains, with a corresponding length of the head. Here was the perfection of the wheat plant, attained according to the well-known physical law, near the most northern limit of its successful growth. Permit me another illustration on the testimony of Professor Maccoun. When at a Hudson Bay post of the region in question — either Fort McMurray, in latitude 57 degrees, or Fort Vermillion in latitude 59 degrees, and about the longitude of Great Salt Lake, an employee of the post invited him to inspect a strange plant in his garden, grown from a few seeds never before seen in that locality. He found cucumber vines planted in April in the open ground, and with the fruit ripened on the 20th of August."

There is a physical cause why wheat grown in the northern region of Manitoba should be superior to that grown in the United States to the south of it. The nearer the northerly limit at which wheat will grow, the finer is its quality. At the northern limit of its growth on this Continent, not only is the soil adapted for it, but the duration of sunshine is longest there when the ears are ripening. From the 15th of June till the 1st of July nearly two hours more daylight prevail in northern Manitoba than in the State of Ohio. It is not heat alone which is required to bring the wheat plant to perfection even in places where the soil is best adapted for its growth. This is true of all grain as well as of all vegetables. Other conditions being present, the greater the amount of solar light the better the result. Now, wheat grown in the Canadian North-West is grown under incomparable advantages with respect to the length of sunlight; hence, that wheat is of the hardest description, is adapted for producing the very finest flour and is certain to prove the most remunerative crop. The acreage suited for the growth of wheat in this region is large enough to furnish bread for the whole of Europe.

## II.

The facts which can be adduced in support of the Canadian Far West being second to no part of the Northern American Continent cannot be gainsaid. It does not follow, however, that every settler there is entirely happy. Many settlers have failed to profit by their opportunities. Some have expected too much; others are unsuccessful because they do too little. There is no royal road to fortune in any new land. In the fairest spot on the earth the hardest worker will reap the richest harvest, while the idler will be unable to earn a living. Last year, the *New York Herald* gave publicity to letters from settlers in Manitoba who complained that the country was utterly unfitted for cultivation. That enterprising journal thereupon dubbed it the "Land of Misery." If the early settlers in Virginia and New England had been men of the same calibre as these grumblers, they would never have developed the resources of Virginia or made New England the home of a prosperous community. The first comers in any undeveloped country are like the first occupants of a new house. The house may be well built, yet it lacks innumerable appliances which render it a comfortable dwelling. The next tenants find it far better fitted for occupation than their predecessors, and every succeeding dweller in it profits by something which has been added to render it more habitable.. So with land which may be capable of growing crops and feeding millions, but which, in its virgin state, is little better than a desert. The next generation will find the Canadian Far West a very different country from what it is to-day. Marshes will have been drained, roads will have been made, railways will be in operation; the soil will yield more abundantly, and the labour of living will be lightened. When its inhabitants hereafter read that it was once styled the " Land of Misery," they will marvel at the credulity, or the ignorance which dictated the phrase.

Eulogy from those personally interested, cannot permanently render a tract of country, which is naturally unsuitable for human beings, a pleasant land wherein to dwell, nor will depreciation on the part of the envious or uninformed hinder a tract, possessing every advantage which Nature can confer, from being appreciated and developed. Unless the Canadian Far West possess all the charms which retain as well as attract settlers, it will relapse into a wilderness over which the savage will again roam and the wild beast multiply. I have no apprehension as to its future. My opinion is based upon what I have beheld. I admit that persons who implicitly trust the fascinating tales circulated by speculators in land may be grievously disappointed. It is as hazardous to buy land anywhere without personal inspection, as it is for a person who has no special knowledge of horseflesh or art to rely upon the assurance of a speculator in horses or pictures. In North America, it is easier to buy land than to sell it. The risk is diminished when the purchaser of land in the Canadian Far West deals with respectable and responsible bodies like the Hudson Bay Company or the Pacific Railway Syndicate, yet in all cases, the purchaser ought to examine his bargain before paying his money. He will display both shrewdness and prudence should he visit the Homestead of 160 acres, which he obtains as a free grant from the Government, before occupying it.

The predominant feeling in my breast as I traversed a part of what the late Earl Beaconsfield termed the "illimitable wilderness" of Western Canada was deep regret that such a region should remain untenanted by busy men. There, year after year the summer sun floods with warmth millions of acres where beautiful prairie flowers bloom and wither, and nutritious grasses spring up and decay. The snows of winter cover the earth with a garment which, though apparently a cold shroud, is really a warm mantle. Game breeds and dies without yielding food to more than a few hunters. Fish spawn and fill the lakes and rivers without being utilized to vary or constitute the subsistence of more than a few Indians. When I thought of the millions of people who might be fed and rear families on the untrodden prairies, and enjoy the game and the fish which abound, it saddened me to contemplate the neglect with which Nature's banquet was treated. And the sadness deepened when I reflected how many landless millions in Europe were struggling for the necessaries of life, or were longing to be the possessors of land which they might call their own, whilst food was easily procurable here by all who might desire it, and land could be had for the asking by all comers. I have seen a large part of the North American Continent. I have marvelled at the enterprise which has converted so much of it from a wilderness into a garden. No other tract can so easily undergo the same transformation as the Canadian Far West. I cannot believe that it will long remain unappreciated and unpeopled.

The result of the settlement of the Canadian Far West will be of paramount importance in shaping the destiny of Canada. Many persons speculate as to the future of the Dominion. The theme is a tempting one, but its adequate discussion is not easy. Confederation dates from the year 1867; the Dominion, as now constituted, dates from the accession of Prince Edward Island in 1873. The settlement of Manitoba, the construction of the Pacific Railway, the opening of steam navigation through Hudson Bay to Europe, are elements of the greatest moment in determining the destiny of Canada, and several years must yet elapse before the influence of these elements is apparent. Men for whom I have the highest respect have pronounced incorporation with the United States to be Canada's inevitable fate. In such a matter as this I hold prediction to be wholly vain. It would not be hard to frame a plausible argument to the effect that the " manifest destiny " of Switzerland was to be absorbed by adjacent and more powerful countries; yet the Swiss entertain no doubt about preserving their independence and they consider that they are fully warranted in so doing. It is clear to my mind that the future of Canada is in the hands of the Canadians. Upon them rests the responsibility, and with them is the opportunity of shaping the issues which determine their destiny. A heavier responsibility or a grander opportunity never fell to the lot of a people. Should they fail in making Canada what it may become, the fault will be their own and not that of their magnificent Far West which, in all physical advantages and potentialities, cannot easily be matched and cannot anywhere be surpassed.

# SUPPLEMENTARY CHAPTER.

### WEEDS IN NORTH AMERICA.

ALL visitors to North America must have marvelled at the luxuriance of the weeds along every roadside. Their number is very great and they are often very beautiful. I wished to write something about them when I met with the following article in the *Union Advocate* of Newcastle, New Brunswick. I think that the readers of this volume will approve of my reprinting the article, and thus enabling them to share in the pleasure with which I perused it and to obtain the information of which it is full.

"The walker makes the acquaintance of all the weeds. They are travellers like himself, the tramps of the vegetable world. They are going east, west, north, south; they walk, they fly, they swim, they steal a ride, they travel by rail, by flood, by wind; they go underground, and they go above, across lots and by the highway. But, like other tramps, they find it safest by the highway; in the fields they are intercepted and cut off, but on the public road, every boy, every passing herd of sheep or cows gives them a lift.

"Ours is a very weedy country because it is a roomy country. Weeds love a wide margin, and they find it here. You shall see more weeds in one day's travel in this country than in a week's journey in Europe. Our culture of the soil is not so close and thorough, our occupancy not so entire and exclusive. The weeds take up with the farmers' leavings, and find good fare. One may see a large slice taken from a field by elecampane, or by teasel, or by milk-weed; whole pastures given up to white-weed, golden-rod, wild carrots, or ox-eye daisies; meadows overrun with bear-weed, and sheep pastures nearly ruined by St. John's wort or the Canada thistle. Our farms are so large and our husbandry so loose that we do not mind these things. By and by we shall clean them out. Weeds seem to thrive here as in no other country. When Sir Joseph Hooker landed in New England a few years ago, he was surprised to find how the European plants flourished there. He found the wild chicory growing far more luxuriantly than he had ever seen it elsewhere, 'forming a tangled mass of stems and branches, studded with torquoise blue blossoms, and covering acres of ground.' This is one of the weeds that Emerson puts in his bouquet, in his 'Humble-bee'—

'Succory to match the sky.'

"Is there not something in our soil and climate

exceptionally favourable to weeds—something harsh, ungenial, sharp-toothed that is akin to them? How woody and rank and fibrous many varieties become, lasting the whole season, and standing up stark and stiff through the deep winter snows—dessicated, preserved by our dry air! Do nettles and thistles bite so sharply in any other country? To know how sharply they bite, of a dry August or September day, take a turn at raking and binding oats with a sprinkling of blind nettles in them. A sprinkling of wasps and hornets would not be much worse.

" Yet it is a fact that all our more pernicious weeds, like our vermin, are of Old World origin. They hold up their heads and assert themselves here, and take their fill of riot and licence; they are avenged for their long years of repression by the stern hand of European agriculture. Until I searched through the botanies I was not aware to what extent we were indebted to Europe for those vegetable Ishmaelites. We have hardly a weed we can call our own; I recall but three that are at all noxious or troublesome, viz.: milk-weed, ragweed, and golden-rod: but who would miss the latter from our fields and highways?

> 'Along the roadside, like the flowers of gold
> That tawny Incas for their gardens wrought,
> Heavy with sunshine droops the golden-rod,'

sings Whittier. In Europe our golden-rod is cultivated in the flower-gardens, as well it might be. The native species is found mainly in the woods, and is much less showy than ours.

" Our milk-weed is tenacious of life; its roots lie deep, as if to get away from the plough, but it seldom infests cultivation crops. Then its stalk is so full of milk and its pod so full of silk that one cannot but ascribe good intentions to it, if it does sometimes overrun the meadow.

> 'In dusty pods the milk-weed
> Its hidden silk has spun.'

sings ' H. H.' in her ' September.'

" Of our rag-weed not much can be set down that is complimentary, except that its name in the botany is *Ambrosia*, food of the gods. It must be the food of the gods if of anything, for, so far as I have observed, nothing terrestrial eats it, not even billygoats. Asthmatic people dread it, and the gardener makes short work of it. It is about the only one of our weeds that follows the plough and the harrow, and except that it is easily destroyed I would suspect it to be an immigrant from the Old World. Our fleabane is a troublesome weed at times, but good husbandry makes short work of it.

" But all the other outlaws of the farm and garden come to us from over the seas; and what a long list it is:—

| | |
|---|---|
| The common thistle, | Elecampane, |
| The Canada thistle, | Plantain, |
| Burdock, | Motherwort, |
| Wild carrot, | Stramonium, |
| Yellow dock, | Catnip, |
| Ox-eye daisy, | Gill, |
| Camomile, | Blue-weed, |
| The mullein, | Stick-weed, |

| | |
|---|---|
| Hound's-tongue, | Mallow, |
| Henbane, | Darnel, |
| Pig-weed, | Poison hemlock, |
| Quitch grass, | Hop clover, |
| Nightshade, | Yarrow, |
| Buttercup, | Wild radish, |
| Dandelion, | Wild parsnip, |
| Shepherd's purse, | Chicory, |
| Wild mustard, | Live-for-ever, |
| St. John's wort, | Toad-flax, |
| Chickweed, | Sheep-sorrel, |
| Purslane, | |

and others less noxious. To offset this list we have given Europe the vilest of all weeds, a parasite that sucks up human blood, tobacco. Now if they catch the Colorado beetle of us, it will go far towards paying them off for the rats and the mice, and for other pests in our houses.

"The most attractive and pretty of the British weeds, as the common daisy, of which the poets have made so much, larkspur, which is a pretty cornfield weed, and the scarlet field-poppy which flowers all summer, and is so taking amid the ripening grain, have not immigrated to our shore. Like a certain sweet rusticity and charm of European rural life, they do not thrive readily under our skies. Our fleabane (*Erigeron Canadensis*) has become a common roadside weed in England, and a few other of our native less known plants have gained a foothold in the Old World.

"Poke-weed is a native American, and what a lusty, royal plant it is! It never invades cultivated fields, but hovers about the borders and looks over the fences like a painted Indian sachem. Thoreau coveted its strong purple stalks for a cane, and the robins eat its dark crimson-juiced berries.

"It is commonly believed that the mullein is indigenous to this country, for have we not heard that it is cultivated in European gardens, and christened the American velvet plant. Yet it too seems to have come over with the pilgrims, and is most abundant in the older parts of the country. It abounds throughout Europe and Asia, and had its economic uses with the ancients. The Greeks made lamp-wicks of its dried leaves, and the Romans dipped its dried stalk in tallow for funeral torches. It affects dry uplands in this country, and as it takes two years to mature, it is not a troublesome weed in cultivated crops. The first year it sits low upon the ground in its coarse flannel and makes ready; if the plough comes along now its career is ended; the second season it starts upward its tall stalk, which in late summer is thickly set with small yellow flowers, and in fall is charged with myriads of fine black seeds. 'As full as a dry mullein stalk of seeds' is equivalent to saying, 'as numerous as the sands upon the seashore.'

"Perhaps the most notable thing about the weeds that have come to us from the Old World when compared with our native species, is their persistence, not to say pugnacity. They fight for the soil; they plant colonies here and there and will not be rooted out. Our native weeds are for the most part shy and harmless, and retreat before cultivation, but the European outlaws follow man like vermin; they hang to his coat skirts, his sheep transport them in their wool, and his cow and horse in tail and mane. As I have before said, it is as with the rats and mice. The American rat is in the woods and is rarely ever seen by woodmen, and the native mouse barely hovers upon the outskirts of civilization; while the Old World species defy our traps and our poison, and have usurped the land. So with the weeds. Take the thistles, for instance; the common and abundant one everywhere, in fields and along highways, is the European species, while the native thistle is much more shy, and is not at all troublesome; indeed, I am not certain that I have ever seen it. The Canada thistle, too, which came to us by way of Canada, what a pest, what a usurper, what a defier of the plough and harrow! I know of but one effectual way to treat it; to put on a pair of buckskin gloves, and pull up every plant that shows itself; this will effect a radical cure in two summers. Of course the plough or the scythe, if not allowed to rest more than a month at a time, will finally conquer it.

"Or take the common St. John's wort (*Hypericum perforatum*), how has it established itself in our fields and become a most pernicious weed, very difficult to extirpate, while the native species are quite rare, and seldom or never invade cultivated fields, being mostly in wet and rocky places. Of Old World origin, too, is the curled leaf dock *(Rumex Crispus)* that is so annoying about one's garden and home meadows, its long tapering root clinging to the soil with such tenacity, that I have pulled upon it till I could see stars without budging it; it has more lives than a cat, making a shift to live when pulled up and laid on top of the ground in the burning summer sun. Our native docks are mostly found in swamps, or near them, and are harmless.

"Purslane, commonly called 'pusley,' and which has given rise to the saying 'as mean as pusley'—of course is not American. A good sample of our native purslane is the Claytonia, or spring beauty, a shy, delicate plant, that opens its rose-coloured flowers in the moist sunny places in the woods or along their borders, so early in the season.

"There are few more obnoxious weeds in cultivated ground than sheep-sorrel, also an Old World plant, while our native wood-sorrel, with its white, delicately-veined flowers, or the variety with yellow-flowers, is quite harmless. The same is true of the mallow, the vetch, or tare and other plants.

"Weeds have this virtue: they are not easily discouraged; they never lose heart entirely; they die game. If they cannot have the best they will take up with the poorest: if fortune is unkind to them to-day, they hope for better luck to-morrow; if they cannot lord it over a corn-hill, they will sit humbly at its foot and accept what comes; in all cases they make the most of their opportunities."

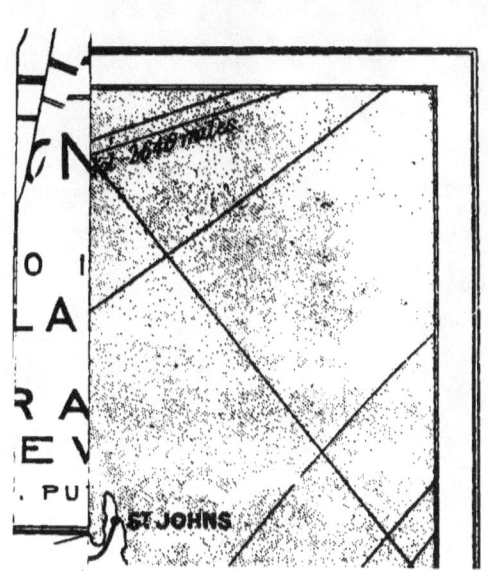

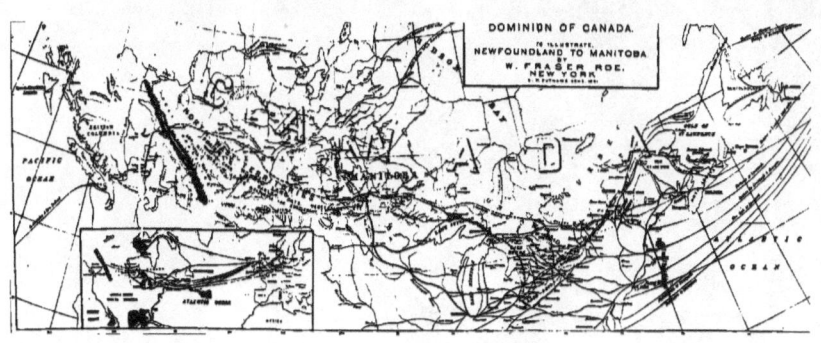

## PUBLICATIONS OF G. P. PUTNAM'S SONS.

**The Round Trip.** By way of Panama through California, Oregon, Nevada, Utah, **Idaho** and **Colorado,** with Notes on Railroads, Commerce, Agriculture, Mining, Scenery and People. By JOHN CODMAN. Octavo, cloth. . . . . . . . . . . 1 50

"This is really an unusually entertaining book of travel, for the author has taken for his 'points of observation' objects and things not often written up and enlarged upon them in an unrestrained, familiar fashion, so that the reader feels as if he were being entertained by letters written for his special benefit by a personal friend."—*Worcester Daily Spy.*

"We have reason to congratulate ourselves, upon the fact that Capt. John Codman has seen fit to weave into literary form some of the best results of his many protracted journeys through the great West, giving them to us in a substantial volume of three hundred and thirty-one pages. The author has made it his special province to go out of the beaten track of those amusement seekers who call themselves tourists, and to see and write rather of the things which tourists do not see at all, or seeing do not understand, than of the conventional 'sights' of the Western States. As he tells us in his preface, 'little is said of large cities, and absolutely nothing of the Yosemite.' For this every reader will be thankful, and the omission can scarcely fail of itself to commend the author's judgment and enhance the reader's good opinion of the book."
—*Evening Post.*

"The writer is a keen observer and possesses the pleasing faculty of presenting his observations in the most vivid manner. The book is one that will undoubtedly attain a wide sale, abounding in matter of the most instructive nature. We heartily recommend its perusal."—*Boston Beacon.*

"A journey of great interest is described in a manner most instructive and entertaining. Captain Codman is a close observer of men and things and a capital narrator. He has a keen sense of humor, a quick eye for picturesque objects and incidents, great skill in catching and preserving local characteristics, and a sensible and racy style."—*Literary World.*

"Mr. Codman has written a remarkably sensible guide-book. It is full of useful information told in a matter-of-fact way. Moral courage is manifested in its opinions, and common-sense in its collection of facts."—*Chicago Times.*

"Books of travel are always interesting when they give us something new, but specially when written in a pleasant style. * * * It is well written, and abounds pleasant and unpleasant incidents and experiences, which are told in a racy and fascinating style."—*Herald & Presbyter, Cincinnati.*

"A narrative of exceeding interest throughout, and replete with instruction. The author is well qualified for his task, and this book has not a dull page in it. It is full of valuable information, and is written in a graphic and highly pleasing style."—*Kansas City Times.*

"It is rare to find a volume of travel in this country so rich and rare. The author, with his trained pen and observant eye, has grouped together a charming picture of travel."—*Pittsburgh Telegraph.*

# RECENT BOOKS OF TRAVEL

**A Lady's Life in the Rocky Mountains.** By ISABELLA BIRD, author of "Six Months in the Sandwich Islands," "A Ride of 700 Miles Through Japan." Second edition, octavo, illustrated, $1 75.

"Of the bold dragoons who have recently figured in military life, bewitching the world with feats of noble horsemanship, the fair Amazon who ides like a Centaur over the roughest passes of the Rocky Mountains will certainly bear away the palm.—*New York Tribune.*

**The Great Fur Land; or Sketches of Life in the Hudson's Bay Territory.** By H. M. ROBINSON. Second edition, octavo, illustrated, $1 75.

" Mr. Robinson's narrative exhibits a freshness and glow of delineation founded on a certain novelty of adventure which commands the attention of the reader, and makes his story as attractive as a romance."—*New York Tribune.*

**The Round Trip,** by way of Panama, through California, Oregon, Nevada, Utah, Idaho, and Colorado, with notes on Railroads, Commerce, Agriculture, Mining, Scenery, and People. By JOHN CODMAN. 12mo, cloth, $1 50.

" No work on California has given a larger amount of useful information than Captain Codman's, and none has equaled his in raciness and general readableness. * * *"—*Literary World.*

**Roman Days.** By VIKTOR RYDBERG, author of 'The Last Athenian.' Translated from the Swedish by A. C. CLARK, with a Biographical Sketch of the Author, by Dr. H. A. W. LINDEHN. 8vo, cloth extra, with twelve plates, $2 00.

"The whole work bears the mark of individual and original thought and research, and is fresh and rich accordingly, and full of new and interesting information."—*Chicago Tribune.*

**Studies of Paris.** By EDMONDO DE AMICIS, author of " Constantinople," " Morocco," " Holland," etc. 16mo, cloth, $1 25.

"A marvel of intense, rapid, graphic and poetic description, by one of the most brilliant of modern Italian authors. The chapters on Hugo and Zola show the same power of description and analysis in dealing with mind and character."—*Christian Register.*

G. P. PUTNAM'S SONS.        New York.

*Cool and Refreshing Reading for the Summer Season.*

**THE GREAT FUR LAND; or Sketches of Life in the Hudson's Bay Territory.** By H. M. ROBINSON, formerly U. S. Assistant Consul in Manitoba. With numerous Illustrations by CHARLES GASCHE. 8vo, cloth extra, $1.75.

A SELECTION FROM THE CONTENTS:

A JOURNEY BY DOG-SLEDGE; CANOE LIFE; THE HALF-BREED VOYAGEUR; THE HUDSON'S BAY COMPANY; LIFE IN A COMPANY'S FORT; A VOYAGE WITH THE VOYAGEURS; THE GREAT FALL HUNTS; THE FRATERNITY OF MEDICINE; THE BLACKFEET INDIANS AT HOME; WINTER TRAVEL; THE FUR HUNTER; A WINTER CAMP; THE FROST KING; A HALF-BREED BULL; A WOOD INDIAN "TRADE."

"Mr. Robinson has admirably succeeded in hitting off the peculiar features of forest life, and in following his graphic sketches the reader is almost made to feel the scent of the odorous woods, and the breath of refreshing air from the breezy mountain-tops. * * * The narrative exhibits a freshness and glow of delineation, founded on a certain novelty of adventure, which commands the attention of the reader, and makes his story as attractive as romance."—*N. Y. Tribune.*

"The Messrs Putnam have published a record of travel and experience in the far North, which, both on the score of novelty of theme and liveliness of treatment may be called one of the most attractive volumes of the season. * * * Altogether, the author has given us a book, which, considering the nature of the information afforded, and the succinctness and spirit of the narrative, is captivating and unique."—*N. Y. Sun.*

"Mr. Robinson's book, it will readily be seen from this, is both an entertaining and instructive one."—*N. Y. Herald.*

"Journeys by dog-sledge, canoe life, the appearance, manners and peculiarities of the half-breed population, the organization of the Hudson's Bay Company, the great buffalo hunt, trading with the Indians, camp life and some other characteristic phases of Northwestern experience are described in a graphic and detailed style, which renders the book very entertaining reading."—*Boston Traveller.*

G. P. PUTNAM'S SONS                        NEW YORK

PUBLICATIONS OF G. P. PUTNAM'S SONS.

BY THE AUTHOR OF "A LADY'S LIFE IN THE ROCKY MOUNTAINS."

**UNBEATEN TRACKS IN JAPAN.** An account of Travels on Horseback in the Interior. By ISABELLA L. BIRD. 2 vols. 8vo. Illustrations and maps. . . . . . . . $5 00

"Of Miss Bird's fascinating and instructive volumes it is impossible to speak in terms of too high praise. They fully maintain the well-earned reputation of the author of 'Six Months in the Sandwich Islands' and 'A Lady's Life in the Rocky Mountains' as a traveller of the first order, and a graphic and picturesque writer. The title she has chosen for her new book is no misnomer. Few foreigners, even of the stronger sex, would have had the courage and perseverance to face and surmount the obstacles which a frail woman in ill health, accompanied only by a single native servant, encountered in her cross-country wanderings. But Miss Bird is a born traveller, fearless, enthusiastic, patient, instructed, knowing as well what as how to describe. No peril daunts her, no prospect of fatigue or discomfort disheartens or repels her,"—*Quarterly Review*, October, 1880.

"Miss Bird is one of the most remarkable travellers of our day. Penetrating into regions wholly unknown by the outside world, she has accomplished, by the force of an indomitable will, aided by great tact and shrewdness, a task to which few men would have been found equal; and she has brought away from the scene of her researches not only a lively tale of adventure, but a great store of fresh and interesting information about the character and habits of a people now undergoing one of the strangest transformations the world has ever seen. We doubt whether the inner life of Japan has ever been better described than in the pregnant pages of this pertinacious Englishwoman."—*N. Y. Daily Tribune.*

"Beyond question, the most valuable and the most interesting of recent books concerning Japanese travel. * * * one of the most profitable of recent travel records."—*N. Y. Evening Post.*

"One of the most readable books of travel of the day."—*N. Y. Daily Times.*

"Miss Bird has given us what to-day must be regarded as the best work on Japan."—*N. Y. Herald.*

"But it is in descriptions of men and manners that she excels, and in these she is so excellent that in no other book in English is there anything like so vivid a picture as she gives of the Japanese people."—*N. Y. World.*

"Her graphic power, her literary skill, and surprising freshness of material, especially in the second volume, make this book one of the very best, and as a work of travels the best, in the library of books relating to Japan."—Rev. WM. E. GRIFFIS, in the *N. Y. Independent.*

"Her narrative is one of intense interest * * * forms a thoroughly valuable and desirable addition to any library."—*Congregationalist.*

"Miss Bird's book is fascinating throughout."—*The American*, Philadelphia.

"She draws out the story of the homely, everyday life in Japan as it has never before been presented."—*The Republican*, Springfield, Mass.

"Japan is truly a wonderful country * * * who follows Miss Bird in its unbeaten tracks will be not only interested, but delighted and almost enchanted. * * * she has told us more about the country, its history, its literature, its business, and the habits, thoughts, and customs of the people, than we might learn from forty ordinary books on Japan * * * a remarkably good book * * * it is brimful of information, much of which has never come under our eye before."—*Boston Post.*

"We do not hesitate to say that of all the books of Japanese travels which we have seen—and we have seen a score or two—this is, without question, the best."—*Louisville Courier-Journal.*

"Among the works of travellers, relating to this country, we are inclined to rank 'Unbeaten Tracks in Japan' as perhaps the best. * * * In all respects it is a sensible, useful work."—*Troy Daily Times.*

"A minute account of the interior of Japan. * * * on nearly every page something new or novel is set forth. * * * This record of life in the interior of Japan is the freshest and most satisfactory of any which has yet been given to the public."—*San Francisco Evening Bulletin.*

# PUBLICATIONS OF G. P. PUTNAM'S SONS.

A NEW VOLUME BY "JOHN LATOUCHE."

**PORTUGAL, OLD AND NEW.** By OSWALD CRAWFURD, British Consul at Oporto. Octavo, with maps and illustrations, cloth extra, . . . . . . . . . $3 50

Mr. Crawfurd, who is better known in literature under his *nom de plume* of John Latouche, has resided for many years in Portugal and has had exceptional opportunities for becoming thoroughly acquainted with the country and its people.

"The whole book, indeed, is excellent, giving the reader not information only, but appreciation of Portugal, its climate, its people and its ways. It is not a book of travel, but a book of residences, if we may say so."—*New York Evening Post.*

"Mr. Crawfurd's admirable book is most opportune, and his long residence in the country, his intimate and critical knowledge of the language, history, poetry, and the inner life of the people, render him an authority as safe to follow as he is pleasant. * * * The book is excellent in every way."—*Athenæum.*

"A more agreeable account of Portugal and the Portuguese could scarcely have been written, and it will surprise us if the book does not live as one of the best descriptions we possess of a foreign nation."—*St. James Gazette.*

**A FORBIDDEN LAND; OR, VOYAGES TO THE COREA.** With full description of the manners, customs, history, etc., of a community of some 16,000,000 people hitherto almost entirely unknown. By ERNST OPPERT. Octavo, with maps and illustrations, $3 00

"The author combines a story of his personal adventures, with a most intelligible description of the country, its inhabitants, their customs, and of everything which would help his readers to form a correct idea of what he himself saw and learned."—*The Churchman.*

"Sure to be eagerly and widely read * * * contains almost the only authentic description of Corea and its people with which the public are familiar."—*San Francisco Bulletin.*

"Full of data of the highest value on the geography and history of Corea, its commercial value and products."—*New York Times.*

"Mr. Oppert has made a book of rare interest."—*New York Evening Post.*

"His personal narrative is one of great interest * * * he is rewarded for his enterprise in being able to communicate so much novel and valuable information in regard to a country which has so long remained beyond the scope of geographical research."—*New York Tribune.*

**ROMAN DAYS.** By VIKTOR RYDBERG. Translated by ALFRED CORNING CLARK, with Memoir of the author by H. A. W. LINDEHN. Octavo, cloth. Illustrated . . . . . . . $2 00

The volume embodies the results of careful historical studies, and gives some legendary matters not heretofore brought forward. The art criticisms are the work of a poet and scholar; the brief historical and topographical sketches, those of a clearheaded philosopher and eager traveller, a quick observer, a man of general and thorough culture. The book is a picturesque mosaic of the many brilliant, sober, gay, comic, dramatic, tragic, poetic, vulgar elements that make up the past history of that wonderful city and the physiognomy it bears to-day.

"We welcome this work from the hardy North for its broad scholarship, its freshness and ripeness. The articles betray an artistic discrimination rare in one not a sculptor by profession and experienced and enthusiastic in that art. Rydberg possesses the pure plastic spirit."—*N. Y. Herald.*

*PUBLICATIONS OF G. P. PUTNAM'S SONS.*

A NEW BOOK BY THE AUTHOR OF "CONSTANTINOPLE."

**HOLLAND AND ITS PEOPLE.** By EDMUNDO DE AMICIS, author of "Constantinople," "Studies of Paris," "Morocco," "Spain," etc. Octavo. With 18 full-page plates. . . . . . $2 00

In this volume of which editions are appearing at once in Florence, Paris, London and New York, the brilliant author of "Paris" and "Constantinople" has turned his steps to a land abounding in picturesque effects and whose history is full of dramatic interest, and his vivid descriptions of the Hollanders and their homes show that his pen has lost none of its eloquence or delicacy of touch. His analysis of the traits and characteristics of this sturdy race, which has played so important a part in the history of Europe, is most interesting and valuable.

"In descriptive passages, Signor Amicis is at home. A wealth of imagery flows from his pen and lightens the pages into prose poems. He has a quiet humor of the Latin type, a disposition to be amused; but he is quick to sympathize with the emotions of his Dutch friends, and if he smiles at their stolidity, admires the rugged qualities and native genius which have produced a William of Orange, a John DeWitt, a Barneveld, and a Rembrandt."—*Boston Traveller.*

"Edmundo de Amicis has transformed the land of dykes into a land of beauty, of wonder, and of enchantment. He has written, in a word, a book in every sense charming."—*Chicago Times.*

"It is only simple justice to say that a more delightful volume of travels hardly may be found."—*Philadelphia Times.*

"His sparkling, graphic book is a thoroughly charming one, to which we give the most unaffected praise."—*Louisville Courier-Journal.*

BY THE SAME AUTHOR.

**CONSTANTINOPLE.** 8vo, cloth, . . . . . $1 50

De Amicis is one of the strongest and most brilliant of the present generation of Italian writers, and this latest work from his pen, as well from the picturesqueness of its descriptions as for its skilful analysis of the traits and characteristics of the medley of races represented in the Turkish capital, possesses an exceptional interest and value.

"The most picturesque and entertaining volume contained in the recent literature on the Eastern question."—*Boston Journal.*

"A remarkable work * * * the author is a poet, an artist, a wonder-worker in words * * * his descriptions are given with rare skill."—*N. Y. Evening Post.*

**STUDIES OF PARIS.** By EDMUNDO DE AMICIS, author of "Constantinople," "Morocco," "Holland," etc. 12mo, cloth extra, $1 25

A series of wonderfully vivid and dramatic pictures of the great world's metropolis, by a writer whose previous books have gained a reputation for exceptional clearness of perception and facility in description. There is hardly a writer who can rival him in his power of reproducing for his readers the very atmosphere of the place he describes. These "Studies" include original and characteristic papers on the two authors whom he considers especially representative of the Paris of to-day—Hugo and Zola.

"Poet in prose, painter in phrases, subtle musician in the harmonies of language, de Amicis has comprehended the manifold amazement, the potent charm of Paris as no writer before him has done."—*Portland Press.*

"A marvel of intense, rapid, graphic and poetic description, by one of the most brilliant of modern Italian writers. The chapters on Hugo and Zola show the same power of description and analysis in dealing with mind and character."—*Christian Register.*

www.ingramcontent.com/pod-product-compliance
Lightning Source LLC
Chambersburg PA
CBHW030754230426
43667CB00007B/962